Talent Optimizer

Why some companies always get great people.

ROB FRIDAY

WWW.ROBFRIDAY.COM

Copyright © 2019 Rob Friday

All rights reserved.

ISBN: 9781692810399

DEDICATION

This book is dedicated to my parents Stephen and Carmela Friday.
You gave me the entrepreneurial spirit.

Contents

Prologue 1

Chapter 1 – Values, Abilities, Skills . . . in that Order 10

Chapter 2 – The cost of a bad hire 20

Chapter 3 – Purpose—Start with Why 30

Chapter 4 – Company Purpose 39

Chapter 5 – Core Values and Beliefs 53

Chapter 6 – Abilities 94

Chapter 7 – Skills 118

Chapter 8 – Desire and Work Values 124

Chapter 9 – Sourcing Talent 129

Chapter 11 – Onboarding and Training 154

Chapter 12 – Culture Champions 163

Chapter 13 – Talent Optimizer Recruiting 182

Chapter 14 – Getting Started 190

About the Author 192

ACKNOWLEDGMENTS

Thank you to all those who helped bring this project to fruition.
My fiancée Jessica, for supporting me to get this done.
Dad, for your guidance and business principles.
Mom, for your support, attention to detail, and assistance editing.
Dave Lahey for taking a chance on me at age 26, for your guidance and mentorship… and for taking the bet that lit the fire to make this happen.
Laura Pratt, for your help with editing and fine-tuning my message.
Thank you to Mike Zani, Daniel Muzquiz, for your inspiration to Play Bigger, along with Dr. Greg Barnett, the team at Predictive Index.
To all my friends, clients, and interviewees who gave so generously of your time and wisdom, including:
Nick Hamm
Dev Basu
Michel Falcon
Vince Tarantini and the team at Carmen Transportation
Dave Dietrich and the team at Erb Group
Phil Strazzulla
Steve Kanellakos
Sulemaan Ahmed
Casey Huebsch
Travis Dutka, Jason Atkins and the team at 360insights
Tuan Nguyen

PROLOGUE

I was twenty-six years old when I started working as a consultant with Predictive Success. It was 2009, and the average age of a consultant working in the Talent Optimization space was over fifty. I very quickly realized I might be in over my head. To be a successful Talent Optimizer, I would need to become an industry expert. I'd need to learn as much as possible about the science and strategy of Talent Optimization. I'd need to become the resource that senior leaders rely on for guidance turning business strategy into business results through people.

I went to work researching the space immediately, eagerly consuming all the information I could get my hands on. At some point during my first year, I came across the following speech. It was delivered on November 3, 1971, by Arnold S. Daniels, the late founder of the Predictive Index® at the Vacuum Metallizers Association's annual meeting. It was more than twenty years before the internet, and Daniels was already speaking about how the nature of labor had changed. This message spoke to me, and it's still among the most important concepts I share with my clients.

Prologue

Arnold S. Daniels' Speech to the Annual Meeting of the Vacuum Metallizers* Association November 3 1971.

Vacuum metalizing is a process used in the application of decorative coatings to a variety of materials.

I have included the speech in its unedited form to preserve Daniels' original message.

Business Management and the Behavioral Sciences

What does behavioral science have to do with business management? Industrial and business operations as we know them today are products of the Industrial Revolution, a system of social change that began to develop about 200 years ago. For 200 years those operations have grown steadily larger, more competitive, and more complex. For most of that time, the behavioral sciences did not exist at all.

The entrepreneur or business manager operating during this period dealt with many of the same general problems we do today. In order to make money he had to invest and risk money in plants, machines, materials, merchandise. They have always recognized the necessity of those investments—and have always done all they could do to minimize their risks.

As their investments—and the risks associated with them—grew larger, science and technology stepped in with sophisticated techniques designed to minimize investment risk. They had to learn them, and to apply them in a landscape that maximized their utilization of the plants, machinery, materials, and money these investments purchased. Calling in the powers of science and technology to managing tangible risks has always been an imperative for the businessperson—and now more than ever.

The other large perennial investment for the businessperson looking to realize a profit on their total investment is labor. In the early days of the Industrial Revolution, the purchase was a fairly simple one. The manager hired "hands" to do the work required to bring his product to market. Indeed, for many years he called these employees simply "hands." The fact that this term has fallen out of use in recent years suggests that there has been a change in the nature of what the businessperson buys with the money they invest in labor.

And while most business people are somewhat aware of that change, few have fully realized the evolving nature of what they're buying when they're buying labor.

What's more, few have yet to fully realize that the purchase of labor is an investment that, like other investments, involves considerable risk—risk that can also be minimized by applying science and technology. In fact, the scientific and technologic innovation available to this category of investment *needs to be* exploited for competitive reasons with every bit the vigor as with the investments made in plants, machinery and materials..

So how has labor evolved over the last two centuries? First, and most obvious, the cost of it has increased steadily. And with the investment in this business fundamental on the climb, it stands to reason that the risks involved have climbed, too.

The nature of the commodity business buys when it buys labor has changed, too. From the simplistic concept of purchasing "hands," I speak about purchasing labor more expansively today. I am referring to the work done by all of the employees of the business at all levels—the sales manager *and* the machine operator. And I speak, too, about the purchase of energy. Or, more exactly, about the purchase of *potential* energy.

To wrap your mind around it, let's get some illumination by way of historical perspective. Let's assume that, back in the early days of the Industrial Revolution, you were the owner of a coal mine, and I worked for you. Whether I liked the work or was well-qualified for it was of no concern to you. Neither was the idea of motivating me to do that work. The fact is, I did it. Difficult and dangerous as it was, I dependably lowered myself into those shafts every day to dig your coal. You didn't have to give a thought to my experience in that job. Because I *had* to do it.

I had to because it was the only way I could feed, clothe, house, and maintain my life and the lives of my family. You controlled my ability to satisfy these basic and essential needs. You didn't have to concern yourself with my fitness for the job or my motivation to do it.

And you not only owned the mine and the tools, you also owned the company house in which I lived, which you rented to me for as long as I worked for you. You owned the company store where I was able to purchase the food and clothing necessary to maintain my family. And you extended credit to me as long as I continued to work for you.

Which I did, because digging coal in your mine was all I *could* do. I had little mobility (I had to stay where I was), I wasn't trained or educated to do anything else, and the labor market was pretty limited.

So, our relationship was a simple one. By giving me a job in your mine, you made it possible for me to satisfy my most essential needs—the only really important needs that motivated me then. If I stopped working for you, I would no longer be able to do that. If I stopped working for you, there would be no institution, no agency, no person who would step up and help me and my family. The dole might be available in time, but it was unreliable and inadequate.

So, you see, I had no alternatives. You purchased my labor—the use of my hands—and I had no recourse but to work for you. I was motivated to do so, and to do it as best as I could, out of fear.

Now, after 200 years of change, the scene is radically changed. Think of me as a worker in your factory today, and consider how different things are. The biggest difference is in the control you, the factory and tool owner, now exercise over my ability to satisfy my basic needs. You are very close now to having completely lost the control that was so firmly in your grasp in the Industrial Revolution. If you fire me, or if I decide I no longer want to work for you (or, for that matter, anyone), I and my family will not be without food, clothing, or shelter.

That's because we have developed a society and cultivated agencies within it that will provide me with these things today, even if I do not work for you or anyone. These provisions guarantee, to a great extent, that I will be able to satisfy my most basic needs. One of the things the behavioural sciences have learned about people is that they are *not* motivated by needs that have been satisfied, or for which satisfaction seems assured. And to further complicate matters, I am today likely to be much better educated than I was 200 years ago. I have much greater mobility. And the labor market is much larger and more varied.

As these changes have occurred, as my needs have changed, my reasons for working have changed, too. This introduces the question of how to get motivated *now*. The behavioral scientists say that my level of motivation has changed, that I have moved up to a higher level in the hierarchy of needs. Motivation at this level is more complex, determined now by a desire for self-respect and respect from my fellows and family, by what I like and want to do, by what kind of person I consider myself.

These considerations had little influence in motivating the 200-year-ago version of me. But if the modern version of me can't find opportunities to satisfy those new needs by working for you, it will simply go elsewhere, where I will have a good chance of finding that satisfaction. Or, and this is more expensive than the cost of turnover should I leave, I may continue to work for you but without interest, enthusiasm, or any sense of involvement, becoming an *underemployed* or perhaps even *unemployed* person *on your payroll.*

It is difficult to measure the exact cost of such a dissatisfied employee, but one of the biggest shrinkers of profit and contributors to inflation is what's known as *psychological underemployment.* If I find my work unsatisfying, uninteresting, discouraging, or frustrating because I am unable to do it well or because it is lacking in social satisfaction, or if I have become cynical about the company or the management for whom I work, or if I am hostile to my boss; or if I am dissatisfied with what I perceive my future to be—then I am psychologically underemployed.

It's a problem that isn't limited to any one business organization or even to business alone. "Such underemployment," said Sir Wilfred Brown, an English entrepreneur, management philosopher, and leader of the Labor Party in the House of Lords, "leads to widespread under-utilization of the potential abilities of millions, without actually depriving them of jobs. I see a direct connection between problems of inequitable wage differentials, underuse of personal capacity, and bad labor relations on one hand . . . and racial intolerance, increasing crime, and a general regression in the behavior of citizens such as is already observable in the US."

Let us return now to the concept that the money you invest in payroll buys only potential energy and the question of what the behavioral sciences have to do with business management. The answer is actually quite simple. The behavioral sciences have developed techniques *you* can use to minimize the risk of your investment in labor, and to assist you in maximizing the utilization of the potential energy you buy with that investment. And again, I remind you that the negative conditions and attitudes that help create underemployment exist at all levels of organizations.

Prologue

The techniques of behavioral sciences can be used, and are used, to improve productivity from the level of the corporation's top management to the level of its production workers. And the problems are at least as acute at the top level as the bottom. Can you estimate how many of the people you know in companies with whom you do business who are dissatisfied, frustrated, discouraged, cynical, and underproductive as a consequence?

Exactly what can behavioral sciences' techniques do for you in the management of your business? For one, they can give you specific, objective measurement of the drives, aptitudes, interests, capacity, motivation, and potential, of both the people you hire and the people already in your organization. Such techniques not only measure but define how and why people work.

I have worked for years with one such technique, the Predictive Index®, and have taught it to my clients so that they can use it in their own organizations. With it, they can predict the specific capacity and potential of anyone relative to any job. It can be applied with equal utilization to the consideration of a potential new hire and the promotion of an experienced employee. It offers unprecedented insight into the motivation of each individual in their organization, an objective and clear understanding of their particular needs.

It also facilitates the identification and definition of an individual's styles of management and communication and offers an understanding of the effect those styles have on individual subordinates.

With it, managers can obtain a clear and objective understanding of the relationships among people in their organizations, and an understanding of how those relationships affect the productivity of individuals and of the organization as a whole.

It can also allow for the early identification of young people whose potential to an organization is meaningful, and provide insight into how to most effectively develop that potential.

And it can eliminate a good deal of the waste, frustration, inefficiency, and turnover that take place when we put people into jobs they are not well-suited to do.

The behavioral sciences are concerned with all aspects of human activity. The Predictive Index®, which is an industrial application of behavioral techniques, is concerned primarily with the behavior of people *in the work environment*. It is a technique for measuring and analyzing that professional space and for defining the demands of jobs of all kinds. With it, it is possible to specifically compare the capacity of a person to the demands of a job, both in terms of the real work environment and by putting him in the job and work environment that maximizes the potential energy he will actually apply to his work, to make him as productive as possible.

To accomplish this, you must really know and understand the person—an imperative techniques like the Predictive Index® make possible. That kind of understanding is basic to motivating your employees in today's real world. There is really not any other way to get at it. To quote a statement on the subject from the May 1970 issue of the magazine, *Supervisory Management*:

"Actually, the only thing a manager can do to achieve better results from subordinates is to establish the sort of climate in his relationships with them that will encourage them to want to move in the direction of achieving organizational goals, while at the same time achieving their own personal goals."

Once your employees have moved beyond the level of basic-need motivation such that you can no longer call or think of them as "hands" (and they long since have), then fully utilizing their energies requires you to understand them as individuals, clearly and objectively. That is a kind of insight into people that very, very few of us can develop without the aid of techniques like those developed by behavioral scientists and made available to management in practical and relatively simple form by way of programs like our Predictive Index®.

Our particular program, by the way, has been designed specifically for use in business. The techniques of measurement it employs are short and efficient, and provide insights into individual capacity, potential, and behavior that would be extremely difficult to obtain in any other way. The program is administered by company management because that is the most efficient way to do it and, more importantly, because only the management of a company has enough real knowledge of its operations, organization, jobs, plans, and objectives to intelligently use the information Predictive Index® generates.

Consultants, who often are stimulating generalists, just don't know enough about specific organizations, specific jobs in those organizations, and the specific problems of real organizations. Our primary function, then, is to conduct a training course in which we teach members of our clients' management teams how and why the Predictive Index® works—and most importantly, *how to use it.*

In doing so, we combine our knowledge, experience, and techniques with management's knowledge of its own business and develop a practical and purposeful program that brings some of behavioral science's basic technology into day-to-day business operation.

Our training course is attended by many people in management who do not often make use of the specific techniques, but who sharpen their managerial skills by gaining the kind of insight into people and their motivations that's taught in the course. We have even had quite a few company presidents complete the course successfully—and benefit from it.

There really is nothing mysterious or obscure about the behavioral sciences. The discipline's focus—the behavior of human beings—is what most of us spend our lives studying and learning about in one way or another anyway. And the information you get from the behavioral sciences and programs like the Predictive index is not so much new as it is *better*, more exactly defined, and more objectively and precisely measured than was ever before possible. And it's better understood than ever before, too.

After all, Hippocrates was analyzing and writing about human behavior in 450 BC and his ideas were interesting, but not useful in any practical sense because he lacked the science and techniques that today translate ideas like his into specific, useful information. And while better understanding of individual behavior and motivation would have been worthwhile at any time in history, there has never before been a time when the need for that understanding has been so urgent and so essential to the maintenance and continued development of this highly productive and complex society we have constructed over thousands of years of trying.

~Arnold S. Daniels November 3, 1971.

Fast forward nearly a half-century, and the challenges Arnold spoke of have only increased. The power the business owner once had over the employee has all but evaporated. The business landscape of the developed world in the digital age is fast-evolving, complex, and often unpredictable. Hiring, engaging, motivating, and retaining today's employee requires a fundamentally different approach—one that isn't for everyone. It takes work, dedication, and a mindset that regards your people as your top priority.

Who this book is for . . . And who should put it down right now!

I think it's prudent to be clear about who this book is designed for. I regularly come across two types of business owners—and only one of them will derive any benefit from this book.

The first type of business owner is looking for a quick fix. They want somebody to give them a silver bullet to "fix" their people. Upon reading Arnold's speech, they would likely wish they were back in the days when they had total control over the coal-miner/employee. They look at spending money on training and developing their people as an expense with a short "shelf life." They spend money on consultants or buy tests and assessments because they think these assessments will tell them something they don't already know. They wish this approach would solve their culture or engagement or management problem.

The second type of business owner recognizes that building a high-performance culture isn't something accomplished overnight. This person understands that developing real, lasting, long-term relationships with their people takes patience and dedication—and that there is no quick fix. These leaders look at spending on their people's training and development as an investment. These leaders are interested in learning how to capture their employees' hearts and minds. They strive to inspire their people and teams to produce to their potential. These leaders want to learn about their employees' natural *strengths* so they can match them to the demands of the position—and the demands of the position to the employees' natural strengths. These leaders want to reap the benefits of this more effective marriage.

So, if you look at training and developing your people as an expense with a short shelf life, there's not much I can do for you. My system is not designed for you, and this book is not for you—don't frustrate yourself!

But if you are looking to invest in yourself and your team, if you wish to learn how to build a lasting, high-performance culture, this book *is* for you. I encourage you to read on.

CHAPTER 1 – VALUES, ABILITIES, SKILLS . . . IN THAT ORDER

"The toughest decisions are people decisions: hiring, firing, and promoting people. They receive the least attention and are the hardest to 'unmake.'"
~ Peter Drucker

Here is a snapshot of the current climate for talent:
- April 2019: US unemployment rate drops to 3.6%.[1]
- 46% of employees stay in a job for fewer than five years.[2]
- One in five employees stays in a job for fewer than two years.[3]
- The cost of an entry-level bad hire is $15,000.
- The cost of an executive-level bad hire is $60,000 to $150,000+.
- Nearly 33% of new hires look for a new job within their first six months on the job.[4]
- 90% of global professionals are interested in hearing about new opportunities.
- The top 10% of job candidates are off the market within ten days.

Over the past ten-plus years of working with hundreds of

companies and thousands of managers, I've seen the competition for talent escalate dramatically. Today's recruiting landscape isn't just more challenging than it was ten or fifteen years ago; it's fundamentally different. The availability of information has shifted the power away from the companies doing recruiting. The power is now in the hands and minds of the candidates. The days of posting ads in the newspaper or hanging a help-wanted sign on the door are long gone. Today's job seekers are savvier than ever. They check Glassdoor.com ratings, read up on company culture, and look for personal growth opportunities. The cost of sourcing, attracting, and retaining top talent is only going up.

To compete in this era, companies are getting creative and offering six-figure salaries and stock options to newly minted MBAs. Others are extending creative and flexible work arrangements, such as work-from-home options, dog-friendly offices, free lunches, and unlimited paid vacations.

All of this can seem overwhelming to the business owner trying to turn a profit—but it doesn't have to be. There is a set of fundamental building blocks that go into creating great cultures full of top talent, and it doesn't start with puppy pee pads in the lunchroom or fully stocked beer fridges.

In this book, I am going to share with you a unique approach to defining, designing, and building an exceptional company culture full of top producers.

I call it the Talent Optimizer Process.

When I share this concept at my seminars for business owners, I explain how these steps will transform their ability to attract, select, and grow top talent. Most business owners understand the concept, and all of them appreciate its power in recruiting and engagement. During these seminars, I tell them that they'll see how these principles have worked for other companies. I say. "You are going to understand that taking these steps will bring you better-quality people. You are going to know deep down that following this process is the right thing to do if you want to fix your recruiting and retention problems. You will take notes, and you will love the ideas, then you will return to your business, and still not implement it."

As you will learn in the abilities section of the book, I know that

Chapter 1 – Values, Abilities, Skills . . . in that Order

most entrepreneurs love a challenge and relish the opportunity to prove someone wrong. So, I challenge these leaders to prove me wrong by implementing this system. To optimize your talent, you need the discipline and determination to step back from the blizzard of working *in* your business and work *on* your business.

When you ask a professional athlete about their ability to deliver excellent game-time performance, they will always talk about the practice and preparation. The same holds for mastery of anything. Sure, God-given gifts can provide a head start for some, but true mastery comes from consistent practice and preparation over time. Tiger Woods didn't become the world's best golfer overnight. He spent thousands of hours on the driving range, hitting millions of golf balls to perfect his swing. If you want world-class results from your company, it will take practice and preparation. So, if you are ready to master the Talent Optimizer process, let's get started.

Think Like a Machine Operator . . . or Optimizer

I want you to think of your business like it's a machine. And to think of each of the people in your business as parts, interacting with the machine. To build the best company possible, you must first design the right machine for creating your products or services. If your machine isn't producing the results you desire, you should step back and determine if its flaw is in the process design or if one of the parts (people) isn't working as it should.

Talent Optimizer Tip: Think like a Machine Optimizer, start by designing the machine needed to deliver your products or services. Think of each position as a part, required to make the machine work.

Using the machine metaphor, you will gain clarity and insight into what makes your business function. Your employees will know precisely what talents they are looking for and how to attract the team they need to help your business grow. While other companies are struggling to work with job boards and recruiting agencies, you will have a self-replicating talent machine, which will bring you unsolicited applications because you've built it to do the work for you. Your people will know exactly how to sift through the applications to identify the type of people who fit your culture and with whom you will want to share your life. You will know precisely how to assess abilities for a particular work. You will ask the right interview questions, listen for the specific answers you need to hear, and probe to separate the actual performers from the pretenders. You will have an ongoing process for evaluating your people. A process that lets you know if things are on track. As chief talent optimizer, you will measure and track the results and, if required, tweak the design of the machine.

Are you happy with the quality of the people you have on your team? Are you satisfied with your managers' abilities to hire people who continually raise the bar of performance in your company? Are you happy with the number of applications you get for the roles you post on your company website? If you leave tomorrow, will your people be able to manage and scale the company with the quality of personnel you know is necessary for executing your vision? Working harder is not the answer. Ping pong tables and bean bag chairs are not the answer. This book offers you a step-by-step, turnkey formula to design and build your very own talent optimization machine.

The Head, Heart, and Briefcase

When I work with clients to implement the talent optimizer process, I share the following model. We call it the head, heart, and briefcase.

Chapter 1 – Values, Abilities, Skills . . . in that Order

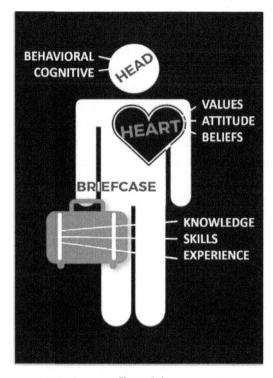

Figure 1-1

- The head consists of the behavioral drives and cognitive abilities the person brings to the job.
- The heart refers to a person's attitude, values, and beliefs.
- The briefcase is the person's knowledge, skills, and experience.

When most companies approach hiring, they focus on the briefcase. What skills are needed to do a job, what knowledge or education do we want the person to bring, and what level of experience is required? This briefcase strategy makes sense because these measures are objective and easy to measure. You can screen for the briefcase assets on a resume or job application. In my experience, over 90% of companies focus here when hiring.

So, what's the problem with this approach? Let's examine it.

When you think about any relationship you've ever had, be it with friends or romantic interests, over time you determined if you were right for each other. When you consider your relationships that have lasted, there is most often a core set of shared values and beliefs that unite you. When personal relationships don't work out, it's usually due to a mismatch of values and beliefs. For example, perhaps you value building relationships and enjoying a vibrant social life, and your significant other prefers to stay home. The chances are good that this mismatch in values will create friction in your relationship. We will go deeper into attitude, values, and beliefs in Chapter 5.

The challenging part here is that we develop our attitude, values, and beliefs over a lifetime. They are inherently personal and mostly fixed. You should not expect to change someone's attitude, values, and beliefs. Dev Basu, a client of mine whom you will meet in Chapter 5, describes values as "factory-installed firmware." If you want to build a great company, you need to figure out which values and beliefs are important to you, and which you are not willing to tolerate. If you get this part wrong, no amount of team-building or leadership development will solve your team dysfunction.

Next, we have the head. The head consists of two parts: cognitive abilities and behavioral drives. As we will explore later, cognitive ability is widely believed to be the most significant predictor of job performance; thus, it is a critical part of the equation. Cognitive ability is, for the most part, a fixed attribute. We either have it, or we don't. So, it's best to determine the requirements for a position and assess your candidates for it.

Behavioral drives predict our needs and thus, the type of work we will find satisfying. Research suggests that these drives develop over the first twenty or so years of our lives. After these drives form, they remain stable. It is important to note that all behavior is a result of a response to stimuli or motivation. Thus, behavioral drives can be adapted. We can do work that we find unsatisfying, temporarily, if we are motivated to do so. However, in the long run, we tend to gravitate toward the activities we find most enjoyable.

This drive to satisfy our needs is why job-slip happens. Someone is hired for a job and initially will do the job precisely as directed. During their probationary period, there is a powerful motivation to keep behaving in a way that's congruent with the job requirements. Then, once the new hire gets comfortable with the role and the company, they start to do things a bit differently. Little by little, they do activities outside their original scope of work, until one day, they are doing something completely different. People are wired to seek pleasure and avoid pain. In the long run, everyone finds a way to satisfy their behavioral needs—so it's best to find out what these needs are, early on, and align them with a role that fits.

Values, Abilities, and Skills Pyramid

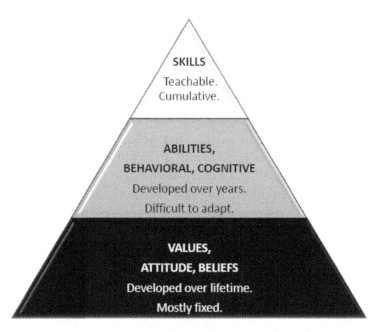

Figure 1-2

Figure 1.2 graphically represents the relative size and malleability of the major traits you will encounter from each employee. You can see the bottom of the figure contains the most inflexible traits, while the top has the most malleable traits. Attitude, personal values, and beliefs are at the foundation—they are the most fixed and must align with the shared values of the leaders of the business. If you find people with shared values and beliefs first, chances are you will always have a place for them in your organization as it grows. If you get the values part wrong, it doesn't matter if the employee has the skills you need or the right mix of behaviors. Incongruent values will cause friction in your business and divide the team. If you have large factions within your business with opposing values, you may have a dysfunctional culture and have difficulty managing some of your major players.

Behaviors and abilities are in the middle of the pyramid, indicating that these traits can be changed temporarily but that one shouldn't expect people to sustain these changes over the long run. Again, it's critical to align natural behaviors and abilities with the work that the position requires.

Finally, skills are at the top of the model. Skills are at the top because they are variable. If you get the lower levels of the pyramid right, you can typically train new skills. With the rate of technology change today, the skills that are currently in demand will likely be outdated in just a few years. Thus, skills are the least important part of the equation when building a robust and sustainable culture. Note: I realize that some jobs require specialized skills. We will discuss skills and how to assess proficiency in Chapter 7. For now, recognize that hiring skills without regard to values and beliefs is a recipe for failure.

Before getting started with the Talent Optimizer process, it's best to set a benchmark by completing the Talent Optimizer Organizational Checkup with the following scorecard. As you implement the process, your score will improve. You can also use this scorecard as an internal review or audit to see if your employees agree with your assessment of your organization.

You can download a copy of the Talent Optimizer Organizational Checkup at www.robfriday.com/TOcheckup

Chapter 1 – Values, Abilities, Skills . . . in that Order

Talent Optimizer Organizational Checkup Scorecard

1. As an organization we encourage each employee to share their personal aspirations and visions for their futures. This policy is understood and embraced by employees at all levels.	0	1	2	3	4	5
2. As a leader I have a clear vision for my future, I know where I want to be in 5-10 years and what steps I need to take to achieve my personal vision. I know my Why and I share it with my employees.	0	1	2	3	4	5
3. As a leader I know the personal aspirations and visions of my direct reports. I know their Whys. I actively take steps to support the development of my people.	0	1	2	3	4	5
4. Our company has a clear company purpose / reason for being / mission. It is aspirational, connects our people to a meaningful cause and it is clearly communicated in writing to all employees.	0	1	2	3	4	5
5. As an organization we have clearly defined, well differentiated core values. These core values are unique to our company, they define what makes our culture different from other companies in our industry.	0	1	2	3	4	5
6. Our core values are clearly understood by all employees. If asked, any random employee will be able to recite the core values on the spot. Our people can give examples of what the values look like in action.	0	1	2	3	4	5
7. Our company culture is part of our brand. We share our company purpose and core values openly with the world on our website and social media channels. Our culture attracts unsolicited applications.	0	1	2	3	4	5
8. As a company we hire, reward, promote and fire based on core values. As a result, all of the people in our company fit with our culture and live our core values.	0	1	2	3	4	5
9. We have a structured interview process complete with a hiring scorecard. We have questions with objective scoring metrics to assess candidates for fit to core values. Our hiring managers are trained to screen for core values.	0	1	2	3	4	5
10. Our company has a validated behavioral assessment solution in place. Senior leadership and hiring managers have been trained on effective use of the solution to support hiring, onboarding and management of employees.	0	1	2	3	4	5

Talent Optimizer Organizational Checkup Scorecard

11. We create behavioral job targets for all roles before we begin recruiting. We use this target to craft a custom job posting for each new position to attract ideal candidates and repel poor fits.	0	1	2	3	4	5
12. We use the behavioral assessment data to guide our structured interview. We have questions with objective scoring metrics to assess job candidates for fit to role	0	1	2	3	4	5
13. All of the people in our organization are in the "right seat" as defined by their abilities and behavioral fit to role.	0	1	2	3	4	5
14. We use skills assessments or assignments with objective scoring metrics to assess for skills proficiency during our hiring process.	0	1	2	3	4	5
15. We actively cultivate a talent pipeline through our company website, about us page, talent community and or social media channels.	0	1	2	3	4	5
16. We have a structured reference checking process for all hires and our hiring managers are trained on how to conduct a structured reference check.	0	1	2	3	4	5
17. We have programs to support living our values and we collect stories of our culture in action. We publish these stories for employees to reference. Example - We have a culture yearbook, or culture slack channel.	0	1	2	3	4	5
18. We have a structured onboarding process to integrate new hires into our culture. New hires sign off on a commitment to live the core values.	0	1	2	3	4	5
19. We have a training program for each new hire complete with checklists and timelines and we conduct ongoing skills training at least twice annually.	0	1	2	3	4	5
20. We have a process/scorecard to track how our leaders and employees live our core values. Our leaders give feedback to our people on how they are living the core values.	0	1	2	3	4	5
Total number for each score 0-5						
Multiply by the number above	x 0	x 1	x 2	x 3	x 4	x 5
Add the above numbers together to determine your current level of Talent Optimization for your company	_____%					

CHAPTER 2 – THE COST OF A BAD HIRE

"We're too busy recruiting to focus on something new."

I heard this objection from an executive at a well-known charity. The reason she felt she was too busy to focus on something new was that the charity was experiencing rampant turnover, with some claiming it was over 65%. In the end, I didn't do business with this organization as it became clear during our discussions that they fell into the first bucket I referred to in the Prologue. They looked at spending money on their people as an expense and focused all of their money and efforts on recruiting new people. There was no budget for onboarding new hires and no process to make the new hires feel welcome. It was evident to any outsider that the charity was caught up in a vicious cycle: New hires were treated with a "trial-by-fire" mentality, and existing employees were disengaged. There's no wonder the Glassdoor.com ratings for the company were terrible and getting worse.

During the time I spent getting to know the organization, I realized that several good people were working there. However, the senior management didn't believe in investing in training and development for their people, and those good people soon left. Since we last spoke, I've heard that things have continued to deteriorate.

What went wrong? For starters, there was no investment in training and no training-and-development strategy to onboard new hires. Worse yet, no one was accountable for ensuring that the newly hired people were what the company needed for the various roles.

What is the Cost of a Hiring Mistake?

If an organization is experiencing a turnover of over 65%, that means that after one year, only one of every three hires is still on board. In the not-for-profit world, this waste is a terrible drain on resources. Further, most charities must maintain specific ratios of expenses to donations to keep their charity standing. The repeated squandering of recruiting and training budgets may threaten its very existence. For a business in the for-profit market, this would be a disaster.

Few mistakes carry a price tag as hefty as the cost of a bad hire. However, many executives don't fully grasp the consequences of making a bad hire. According to a 2017 CareerBuilder survey, "companies lost an average of $14,900 on every bad hire in the last year, and it's a common mistake—nearly three in four employers (74%) say they've hired the wrong person for a position."

[5] Further, the impact of a bad hire cascades throughout the rest of the team and organization, lowering the overall performance and causing other high-potential employees to leave. According to the same study, employers believe "the average cost of losing a good hire was $29,600 this year." Estimates for executive-level positions range from two times the base salary up to over six times the base salary. If a senior executive makes $175,000 per year, this puts the estimated cost of a bad hire at $350,000 up to $1.05M.

Why Are Hiring Mistakes So Expensive?

Think about the last time you worked with a disengaged employee. Take a moment and consider how that employee's attitude and performance affected you. Chances are your blood pressure went up just thinking about it.

The impact of a bad hire goes far beyond the hard costs of recruiting and hiring. Gallup puts the cost of a disengaged employee at $3,400 per $10,000 of base salary—or 34% of base salary per year.

Chapter 2 – The Cost of a Bad Hire

This estimate means an employee earning $60,000 a year costs the company just over $20,000 a year in forfeited opportunities.

The hard costs of job postings, recruiter salary, and training are easy to quantify. Calculating the indirect costs of a hiring mistake can be more complicated. Here are some of the indirect costs that I've seen bad hires levy on businesses during my time working with clients:

- Lost customers due to poor customer service;
- Lost sales due to a lack of follow-up or the underperformance of bad or lazy sales reps;
- Disengagement and turnover among other employees affected by the bad hire;
- Lower overall team performance;
- The loss of intellectual capital due to other employees leaving;
- The opportunity cost of losing other high-potential employees;
- Overtime and additional workloads levied on the rest of the team to compensate for the poor performer's lack of contribution;
- The increased costs of recruiting new employees due to the impact on the employer's brand, Glassdoor, and online ratings;
- The impact of turnover issues on the recruiting and human resources team;
- Negative industry visibility;
- Negative press;
- Ramp-up and training time for new hires.

Also consider the damage that poorly selected employees' decisions can have on the company. In the case of very senior executives with significant decision-making authority, the results can be catastrophic.

The bottom line is that hiring is a significant investment—one that is best treated with the same consideration as any other significant capital expenditure. Moreover, where very senior hires with decision-making responsibilities are concerned, the stakes for the company can be surprisingly high.

Impact of A vs. B Players

Should I keep my B Players? This is a question I get frequently. What should I do about the B Players on my team? They produce adequate results; they don't complain about pay like the A Players do, but they don't often deliver above minimally acceptable levels. Do we keep, cut, or coerce?

The answer is: it depends.

First, examine the macro factors that impact your business. Are you in a high-growth industry in which the B Players' performance might cost you market share that you can never get back? Will their lack of performance allow your competition to beat you to market? Will the B Players' impact on your burn rate put the company's financial sustainability at risk? Does their mediocre performance rob the company of sales and recurring revenue? Are they responsible for leading a team that will produce sub-optimal results? If the answer to any of these questions is yes, the B Player must go to make way for an A Player.

If, on the other hand, you are in a stable or moderate-growth industry, the impact of a B Player might not be as significant. In these situations, you might look at the individual or micro factors surrounding the B Player.

Next, examine the micro factors. What type of work is the B Player doing? Are there options for replacing the B Player with an A Player? If you have a B Player in an individual contributor role with minimal impact on your overall business, this might be OK. The effect of a B Player in a position that requires manual labor will never be as significant as the impact of a B Player in a leadership role or a role that uses leverage.

 Talent Optimizer Tip: Do not tolerate average performance in high-growth, high-tech, or recurring-revenue businesses.

Manual Labor Roles

These are the lowest-skilled roles and typically require the least amount of training. Think grocery-store cashier, shelf stocker, cleaner/janitor, construction worker, and general laborer. The top performers in these roles rarely exceed one-and-a-half to two times

Chapter 2 – The Cost of a Bad Hire

the performance of the average.

Procedural Roles

In procedural roles such as bookkeeping, data entry, and graphic editing, the best are typically about two times as effective as the average players. These people are often easy to replace, and training isn't challenging because the procedures have a defined process and a single defined correct outcome.

These lower-skilled roles are also easy to replace with technology support or outsourcing with virtual freelance services like Upwork.
https://www.upwork.com/

There are also new services popping up in this space all the time. I recently came across TopTal, which claims to screen freelancers to find the top 3% available. I've heard great reviews of this site for non-tech savvy entrepreneurs in need of developers and programmers.
https://www.toptal.com

Sales

In customer/client-success roles, the top performers are generally about two times as effective as the average. This is a modification of a procedural job as there is typically a defined process, and variance should be somewhat minimal.

In inside sales roles with inbound leads, the best sales reps are typically between two and four times as effective as average players. Monitoring lead count and closing ratios easily quantify this. These metrics are also a good comparison to use for recruiting roles.

In outside sales "hunter" roles, the difference can be much more significant—often five times and up to ten times or even more. When outside sales reps are responsible for generating leads, A Players' performance vastly outperforms the average. Working smarter, not harder, earns big rewards.

When thinking about sales roles, it is essential to account for the lifetime value of a customer in industries with recurring revenue components to the sale, such as software sales. Here, it is best if you consider the present value of the projected spend over the customer's lifetime. If you have average performers wasting leads by not calling customers back or ineffectively presenting your products and services, you are wasting time, which is money. It's often hard to give up on persuasive, likable salespeople. However, the opportunity cost of not replacing these sales reps with A Players—in high-growth or recurring-revenue businesses—is too great.

Creative and Innovative Roles

In roles with no defined processes and many possible correct answers, the results from the best performers can be ten times better than those from the average, or more. You must also consider the impact of "brilliant jerks" in these individual contributor situations, such as outsourced copywriters or computer programmers. In these limited circumstances, the "brilliant jerk" may be appropriate so long as their interactions with the team are controlled and limited. If, however, the "brilliant jerk" is expected to contribute to a team, this is a recipe for disaster. Team chemistry and cohesion trump the contributions of any one person. Don't expect a team to perform at a high level when one of its members is toxic. No matter how effective the skills or talent of the person(s) concerned might be, if teamwork is required, do not consider the "brilliant jerks" in creative or innovative roles.

 Talent Optimizer Tip: No matter how effective the skills or talent, if teamwork is required, do not consider the "brilliant jerks" in creative or innovative roles.

Computer Science and Programming

In the book *Work Rules!*, Laszlo Bock shares Google's philosophy on performance and compensation. He shares that some "Googlers[1]" receive compensation a thousand times that of others doing similar jobs. This variance is because the very best computer programmers are a thousand times or more as effective and productive as the

---

[1] Term for Google employee

average programmer.

Leadership Roles

Consider the value of an individual contributor on a team of five people. Holding other factors constant, if the individual contributor increases their performance by 20%, the group as a whole becomes 4% more productive.

120% + 100% + 100% + 100% + 100% = 520%
520% / 5 = 104%

If, on the other hand, the leader is 20% more effective at getting results out of each team member, the team will realize the full 20% increase in performance. As organizations grow and multiple layers of management form, the impact of a senior leader's effectiveness at getting results from subordinates grows exponentially.

Pay "Unfairly"

In low-tech organizations with large amounts of manual labor, it is not possible to have one employee outperforming others by a factor of ten. In these industries, performance is generally normally distributed. Thus, compensation should be normally distributed, too. Reward the top performers more than the average, but the gap should rarely be over one-and-a-half to two times.

In high-tech, high-growth, or recurring-revenue businesses, the top performers will generate ten to 1,000 times the results of the average ones. As Laszlo Bock explores in *Work Rules!*, in these cases, you *must* pay unfairly to avoid losing your best people. A policy of pay equity in this type of environment will incentivize your best people to leave for other opportunities. If you are a young or cash-strapped company, consider stock options. If you are on a fixed budget, take from the B Players and reallocate to the A Players; it's the only fair thing to do.

What is the Value of Your Company Brand Equity?

In her book *Powerful: Building a Culture of Freedom and*

Responsibility, author Patty McCord explains how Netflix approaches pay and compensation. She brings to light the importance of considering the specialized skills, experience, and value employees develop while at your company. In one instance at Netflix, an employee was working on a very specialized matching algorithm. No one else in the world had this type of experience. This ultra-specialized skill made him incredibly valuable to the competition and warranted a massive pay increase. Patty explains that Netflix initially opposed the pay increase, but after considering the impact of losing the team, they elected to double the salary of all employees working on the project. She goes on to make the point that Netflix focuses on being a great place to be "from," meaning they expect employees will leave over time, but they want to be respected as an excellent place for people to learn and develop their careers.

Why Do Companies Get Hiring Wrong?

If the costs of a mistake are so high, why do companies continue to get this wrong? In my experience, there are several reasons.
1. Hiring is a subjective and ad-hoc process left up to managers with little oversight;
2. The team doesn't do a good job assessing for fit to the team, job, manager, or company culture;
3. The person responsible for the new hire doesn't have clarity as to what they are looking for;
4. The new employee doesn't have the required skills and is not given sufficient time to acquire them;
5. The team is stretched and makes a hiring decision too quickly.

How to Ensure Against a Hiring Mistake

When an accountant looks at the purchase of a new piece of machinery, the process involves looking at the available alternatives, calculating a payback period, and determining whether the investment makes sense for the business. If employees' salaries are the largest investments that most companies make every year, doesn't it make sense that there should be a similar process for evaluating these investments?

Chapter 2 – The Cost of a Bad Hire

Considering the five reasons for hiring mistakes listed above, establishing a process upfront to ensure against making mistakes seems like a logical first step to improving results.

In the chapters that follow, we will:
1. Bring structure and objectivity to the recruiting process;
2. Define what the fit to team, role, manager, and company culture look like;
3. Learn how to identify the values, purpose, behaviors, abilities, and skills of the ideal employee;
4. Learn techniques for assessing skills proficiency and learning ability;
5. Establish a repeatable, scalable, and objectively measurable system to bring in top-tier talent;
6. Learn how to design, hire and inspire people to turn your business strategy into business results.
7. Learn how to conduct a 5-step reference check
8. Learn best practices for onboarding and training
9. Learn how to maintain a healthy culture.

Chapter 2 Action Steps

Think about the last bad hire(s) you made or worked with and consider the five questions below to determine where you went wrong.

1. Was the hiring subjective and ad hoc, having been left up to managers with little oversight?

2. Did the team do an adequate job assessing for:

    a. fit to the team
    b. fit to the role
    c. fit to the manager
    d. fit to the company culture?

3. Did the person or team responsible for the new hire have a clear picture of what they were looking for? Which of the following were the most significant issues?

a. values
   b. purpose
   c. behaviors
   d. abilities
   e. skills

4. Did the hiring team assess the required skills and learning abilities?

5. Did the hiring team use a structured system that allowed for post-mortem diagnosis and measurement?

After answering these five questions, which areas do you conclude need addressing?

CHAPTER 3 – PURPOSE—START WITH WHY

"People don't buy what you do; they buy why you do it. And what you do simply proves what you believe."
~ Simon Sinek

The Entrepreneurial Itch

I've had the entrepreneurial itch for as long as I can remember. Growing up, I was that kid knocking on the neighbors' doors offering to shovel their driveway for five bucks. When I was in high school, I started a business by making Muskoka chairs in shop class and selling them at local flea markets on the weekends. I credit my parents for supporting my creativity and installing the entrepreneurial drive in me from a young age.

My dad, Stephen Friday, is a life-long entrepreneur, too. While I was growing up, he owned a series of different businesses in a variety of industries. I recall one of his entrepreneurial principles:

"Find something you love to do, get someone to pay you to learn the business, then buy that business or start one just like it."
~ Stephen Friday

contributions daily.

Third, the team reviewed all 15,000 comments and suggestions and boiled things down to four themes:

- Back to basics—Employees felt there was too much red tape, too many layers of decision-making, and too much bureaucracy. People were not empowered to respond to issues in a reasonable amount of time.
- Communication and engagement—Employees felt there wasn't enough communication about organizational direction and not enough input in seeking to improve the workplace and services.
- Personal development for staff—There was a lack of training and development opportunities. The city needed to invest in its people, give them the training and tools required to meet their personal and career goals, become more effective leaders, and help others become more successful.
- Continuous improvement of services—There wasn't enough investment in digital systems and process improvement. Employees wanted to provide better service but were frustrated at the lack of tools and support provided.

The first category was addressed immediately. Steve and his team eliminated the red tape, allowing both employees and citizens increased access to members of the council and reducing the decision-making bureaucracy at every level.

To address categories two, three, and four, Steve began with "servant leadership."

What is servant leadership?

It is, Steve explains, a set of behaviors and practices that turn the traditional "power leadership" model upside down. "Instead of the people working to serve the leader, the leader exists to serve the people. As a result, the practice is centered on a desire to serve and emphasizes collaboration, trust, empathy, and the ethical use of power. Its primary goal is to enhance individual growth, teamwork, and overall employee involvement and satisfaction."[7]

Steve took this approach to heart, identifying the leaders in the organization who embodied this servant-leadership mentality, and created a leadership philosophy based on four pillars.

The Four Pillars

1. Leadership development: The city has a "people plan" and invests in the systems and tools to determine who can do what in the future to maintain a strong leadership pipeline.
2. Learning and development: The city invests in training and personal development opportunities for its people, ensuring employees develop the knowledge, skills, and competencies to meet their personal and career development goals.
3. Performance management: The city has a process for performance feedback and management. Employees regularly receive coaching and feedback from managers. Employees are encouraged to provide input and feedback.
4. Succession management: The city has clearly defined succession paths and development plans to help employees build a career with the city.

These four pillars work together to create a people-first culture where employees see a future for themselves. They see the career paths and development plans that are necessary to help them achieve their personal goals.

Implementation

This type of initiative needs to come from the top down. Steve started by showing the managers the servant-leadership approach. Next, he implemented the Predictive Index® system to help managers have coaching conversations and make development plans more objective. By defining the requirements of a role and identifying the natural gaps that exist, development conversations are more concrete and factual. Starting these reviews and coaching interviews with real objective data lowered the threat level. People were open to feedback and genuinely interested in their personal development.

When discussing this implementation with employee stakeholders, the decision boiled down to the performance review and development plans. Would the employees rather these discussions and plans be based on subjective manager opinions or supported with objective data? In the end, the objective data was the clear winner.

The Results

Twenty-four months into this transformation, there has been a

CHAPTER 6 – ABILITIES

Why Abilities?

I use the term "abilities" because I want to capture all types of abilities. Let's, for a moment, consider the example of a superhero. Every superhero has unique abilities that give them an edge. It might be superhuman strength, or perhaps X-ray vision or the ability to fly or read thoughts. Each of these abilities carries with it a unique set of circumstances where they will come in handy. Every superhero movie finds a way to create a situation that requires a unique ability to save the day.

Now, let's think about real-life applications. Every person has a unique set of abilities. Some of them might be natural; others may be developed over time. These might include the ability to run long distances, lift 500 pounds, dunk a basketball, quickly calculate complex math problems mentally, speak multiple languages, recognize intricate patterns, think laterally or linearly, persuade and influence, maintain focus for long periods of time, deal with conflict effectively, work quickly, maintain a calm demeanor in high-stress situations, and so on.

One of the defining characteristics of abilities is that they are difficult—and, in some cases, impossible—to develop. If I am five feet tall, it doesn't matter how hard I work; it will be virtually impossible for me to dunk a basketball. Ability implies that one has

Chapter 6 – Abilities

the means, talent, or skill to do something. It also implies that others will not have the same means, talent, or skill.

Now think about how this applies to business and the design of your machine. For every position in a company, there are required abilities needed to do the job effectively.

A center on an NBA basketball team will require abilities related to height and endurance, along with abilities tied to teamwork, communication, and stress management.

A line chef at a high-end restaurant will require the ability to maintain focus for long periods of time, will have great attention to detail, and will be able to follow instructions carefully.

An outside sales position will require the ability to communicate persuasively. Also, a person in that position will need to deal well with conflict and rejection and manage multiple activities concurrently.

An accountant will need abilities related to being detail-oriented, thinking analytically, following rules, and doing repetitive work.

Some of the abilities required for each of these jobs are related to physical abilities; others are mental abilities; and others are behavioral in nature.

In my experience, this is another critical step at which most organizations stumble. They fail to define the abilities required for a given role accurately, and they fail to assess candidates against the required abilities effectively.

Thinking back to the machine metaphor, we first design the machine and identify the required parts. By defining the requirements for each role in an organization, business managers gain an objective way of assessing if they have the right people in the right spots. Further, they reduce the chances of promoting or moving someone into the wrong role.

We typically approach this step in two parts.

> Step One: Define the behavioral requirements of the role.
> Step Two: Define the cognitive requirements of the role.

Behavioral Job Requirements

These are attributes of what is generally known as "personality."

Unfortunately, these attributes are very difficult to judge accurately, particularly during an initial meeting with an individual. The knowledge gained from experience working with an individual over time would be helpful. Unfortunately, such knowledge is often simply not available to the manager and decision-maker. I refer to a very long list of attributes such as: initiative, assertiveness, sense of urgency, judgement, empathy, patience, respect for authority, adaptability, self-confidence, decisiveness, attention to detail, cooperativeness, openness to change and new ideas, response to pressure, conflict or rejection, pace of learning, independence, risk-taking drive or caution/risk-avoidance, need for close support and assurance of security or need for opportunity for self-expression, and so on.

In every job and career, some combination of those attributes is critical to success. No one individual can be all of those things, and no one job involves all of those attributes. But some of those attributes define the personality of every individual, and some of them define the requirements of every job.

What's more, these attributes explain and predict the difference between outstanding, average, and poor performance—the difference between success and failure.

All of this brings us to the big question: How do you get accurate, objective, and specific information about your people and their potential? How do you get the type of information needed to design, hire, and inspire the kind of people you require to turn your business strategy into business results and achieve your vision?

This is what I spend a great deal of my consulting time helping companies implement. The system is called the Predictive Index®.

The Predictive Index®

Predictive Index® was founded in 1955 by Arnold S. Daniels. Daniels was a bombardier, navigator, and gunnery officer in the United States Army Air Force in the 1940s. During the Second World War, Daniels flew over 30 missions. The average mortality rate for bombardiers was in the range of 50%, so with over thirty

Chapter 6 – Abilities

successful missions, Daniels's team was an anomaly. During this time, the U.S. Army Air Force was conducting a study of successful teams. Daniels was assigned a psychologist to work with assessing the composition of these teams. He was fascinated with the idea that a simple assessment could save your life in combat situations. He subsequently made it his life's purpose to bring these scientific techniques to the business world. After being discharged from the army, Daniels studied workplace psychology in Boston, working with management consulting firms, and attending Harvard Business School. In 1955, he released the first Predictive Index® behavioral assessment to the business world and paired it with a five-day leadership-training program.

Over the past sixty-plus years, the Predictive Index® has undergone five science updates. The most recent in 2016 under the leadership of CEO, Mike Zani, President & Chairman, Daniel Muzquiz and Vice President, Science Dr. Greg Barnett.

Today, the Predictive Index® is a cloud-based software as a service (SAAS) technology company with a rigorous scientific background. Zani and Muzquiz have invested heavily in revalidating and refining the science, while continually developing world-class Talent Optimization software.

How Does the Predictive Index® Work?

Based on research initially published in *Emotions of Normal People* by William Moulton Marston in 1928, the Predictive Index® behavioral assessment measures four core behavioral drives and two secondary constructs using a free-choice checklist methodology. Today, as in 1955, assessment takers are presented with a list of behavioral stimuli in the form of adjectives, and they are instructed to answer two simple questions. Pick those you feel describe the way you are expected to act by others, then pick those you feel describe you. The results are scored in four main categories that correspond to the four main behavioral drives that all adult humans have.

Dominance: The drive to exert one's influence on people and events.
Extroversion: The drive for social interaction with other people.
Patience: The drive for consistency and stability.

Formality: The drive to conform to rules and structure.

The first secondary construct, titled E, is a measure of decision-making preference—it indicates a preference for objectivity and facts or subjectivity and intuition in decision-making.
The final construct, M, is a measure of responsiveness to the Predictive Index® assessment.

When an individual takes the free-choice[3] survey, the results are scored on a bell curve that compares their responses against the normal range of the adult working population. This methodology allows for a comparison of high, medium, and low levels of each behavioral drive. "Typically, benchmarked samples only allow you to see how someone falls on a spectrum relative to others in the working population. While the Predictive Index® Behavioral Assessment leverages this benchmarking methodology, it also reaches beyond typical people-to-people differences to provide a lens into people's distinct drives and needs by a comparison of behavioral factors."[2]

For example, two people may have similar levels of extroversion; however, one person may have a higher level of formality relative to the level of extroversion while the other may have a low level of formality compared to the level of extroversion. In this example, the relational difference between the levels of extroversion and formality will explain and predict how their different sets of drives and needs will impact workplace behavior. The free-choice aspect of the Predictive Index® assessment allows for an advanced level of insight and analysis that is not possible when using a forced-choice[4] assessment.

Drives, Needs, Behaviors

I've always been fascinated by the concept of behavior—why people behave the way they do and why two people presented with

---

[3] Free Choice: A testing methodology in which test takers may choose their responses from a large set of possible options. This methodology has many possible combinations of responses. Predictive Index® is an example of a free-choice assessment.
[4] Forced-Choice assessment – A testing methodology in which test takers must select a response from two or more available choices. This methodology has a fixed number of possible responses. The DISC assessment is an example of a fixed-choice assessment.

Chapter 6 – Abilities

the same situation will react in entirely different ways. I've spent a great deal of time learning about this, researching various theories and perspectives. We will never fully resolve the nature-versus-nurture debate. Based on my research, I am going to share my thinking on the topic to the best of my current understanding.

"Tabula rasa" is a term often used in psychology to describe the state of a newborn baby. Thought to date back to the Roman's "tabula" for note-taking, it translates as "blank slate." As we humans grow up, we experience a variety of different types of situations, also known as stimuli. Our experiences in dealing with these situations develop our mental models for how the world works. As we learn how to deal with situations, our brain develops neural pathways that allow us to respond to most daily ones on virtual autopilot. This pattern recognition is among the many unique features of the human brain that enable us to function at higher levels. As we deal with these situations, again and again, these patterns repeat themselves, and our responses become more and more ingrained. By about age twenty, our behavioral drives are mostly formed, which means our understanding of the way things work is pretty well developed. Thus, if we hold all other things equal, someone will feel the same behavioral drives and needs at age twenty as at age thirty, forty, or seventy-five. This doesn't mean we will always behave similarly. It means that we will experience the same underlying needs that motivate us to want to behave similarly.

To explain this in a model, consider the following: People develop their behavioral drives, dominance, extroversion, patience, and formality through the first 20 years of life; after age 20, the drives are formed. As a result of these drives, people will express a particular set of needs. Because the drives are fixed, the associated needs are also fixed. All behavior is a result of stimuli and motivation. Unless there is a strong motivator to the contrary, all things being equal, people will behave in a way that satisfies their needs. Thus, people have drives. Drives create needs. People behave in a way that satisfies their needs.

Now, if you don't have a way of measuring the drives, the only thing you have to base your decisions on is observation. The only thing you can observe is behavior. And if you are only observing behavior, you are guessing at the underlying drives and needs. Because behavior is a response to stimuli and motivation, we often get fooled. People sometimes behave in ways that are incongruent with their underlying needs for periods of time, when there is a strong motivator or stimuli to the contrary.

For example, consider a job interview. If a candidate wants a job, they will behave in ways that are most congruent with what they believe the company is seeking. If hired, they have a strong motivator for the first ninety days to continue behaving this way to ensure they pass their probationary period. As I am sure many of you have experienced, over time, people start to behave differently. Once comfortable, their true colors begin to show, and these people gradually revert to doing what they find most satisfying. This phenomenon explains why so many companies experience a challenge with employees after the probationary period is up. With the help of assessments and systems like the Predictive Index®, business leaders can gain insights into what type of work people will find most satisfying. They can use these insights to align employees' needs to the role from the outset.

To understand this a bit more thoroughly, consider the following deep dive on drives, needs, and behaviors.

Drive	**Needs** *(what people need)*	**Behaviors** *(expected behaviors)*
High Dominance	Independence To be challenged	Assertive Self-confident
Low Dominance	Support Freedom from conflict	Agreeable Accommodating
High Extraversion	To talk things out Social Interaction	Outgoing Persuasive
Low Extraversion	Time to think Privacy	Serious Task-oriented
High Patience	Time to practice Stability	Patient Deliberate
Low Patience	Variety To take action	Fast-paced Intense
High Formality	Rules Structure	Organized Precise
Low Formality	Flexibility To try new methods	Informal Casual

Table 6-1

Chapter 6 – Abilities

No one person possesses or prefers all these behaviors or qualities, and no one job requires all of them. However, each person does possess some of these behaviors, and each role does require some of these characteristics. The task then is to identify the behaviors required for each role and the people best suited to perform them.

It's All About the Fit

When contemplating how a candidate or employee will fit into a given situation, the following four essential areas must be considered:
1. Fit with the role
2. Fit with the manager
3. Fit with the team
4. Fit with the organization or culture

Fit with the Role

When considering an individual's fit to a role, the first step is to define the requirements of the role. The first and best way to define a role is through the analysis of real data. If a company has a sufficiently large group of top performers, using a validated assessment like the Predictive Index® can provide a benchmark against which to compare future hires. If no group of high performers exists, the next best alternative involves surveying a group of stakeholders that understand and agree on the requirements of the role. Use a job diagnostic like the Predictive Index® job assessment and determine the factors that will drive success. In August 2019, the Predictive Index® announced a new job posting analyzer. This tool uses machine learning to give hiring teams a suggested behavioral target based on the language used in the job posting.

Starting with a benchmark allows the manager making the hiring decision to ask the candidate more direct questions. They can dig into their past performance to determine if they have been able to effectively display the behaviors and abilities required for the given position. Remember that, in the long run, it's best to align the individual's underlying needs with the needs of the job.

Once an individual is in the role, this information is incredibly valuable for providing coaching, development, and feedback.

Employees are often more open to this style of objective feedback. It also lowers the threat level as it's not the manager's opinion of the employee; it's the data from the assessment.

Fit with the Manager

I firmly believe that people join an organization, but they leave a manager. Understanding an individual's fit to a manager is the second-most vital fit to consider. When an employee comes to work, they work in an environment that is most influenced by their manager.

Talent Optimizer Key Point: When an employee comes to work, they work in an environment that is most influenced by their manager.

If the manager understands the employee's needs, they can provide coaching and feedback in a way that works well for the employee. The golden rule of treating others as you would like to be treated is, in fact, not all that effective. The platinum rule of treating others as they themselves *need* to be treated is more effective for driving long-term performance and job satisfaction. For managers to effectively implement this, it is vitally important that they understand and appreciate the differences each person brings to the team. By paying close attention to the different needs of each employee, a manager can effectively create an environment in which the employees can do their best work. I love using the example of the famous duck/rabbit[12] image.

Chapter 6 – Abilities

Figure 6-1

When you look at this image, your mind instantly filters it based on your mental model of how the world works. You either filter the picture as a rabbit or as a duck. When I use this graphic in my keynotes, I usually get about a fifty-fifty rabbit-duck split. It makes no difference which one you see first; the important thing is that you are regarding the same stimuli, but your mind filters it differently. I then explain how the science of stimulus-response works. Two people may experience the same situation, but their mental models will cause them to respond in two completely different ways. This difference in response is a result of how our minds are wired. It's impossible to experience reality in exactly the same way as someone whose behavioral profile is the opposite of yours.

Managers can learn to understand these differences and acknowledge that they exist. They can even start to adapt their management approach to engage and motivate people who are different from them more effectively. But it's still impossible to experience things from another person's point of view.

To drive this home, I love using an example that Ray Dalio referenced in his book *Principles*.

"Imagine trying to explain what a rose smells like to someone who does not have a sense of smell. No matter how good your explanation is, it is no substitute for the real thing."[13]

This analogy resonates with me. The fact is that it's impossible to experience reality from another person's point of view if it is different from your own. Keeping this in mind when managing others who are different from you is critical to driving and maintaining performance.

Talent Optimizer Key Point: It's impossible to experience reality from another person's point of view if it is different from your own.

Fit with the Team

The third fit to consider is an individual's fit to the team. As the speed of innovation increases and organizations are increasingly dependent on knowledge workers, individual specializations are required, but only if they can be effectively utilized in a team format. Thus, teams must understand and appreciate the differences among their members. If a team member feels alienated or intimidated, they will not produce optimal results. One of the first steps teams should take when starting a new project is to look at the profiles of the other team members. Discuss the implications of how the individuals will work together. What are the team's natural areas of strength? Do they align with the goals the team is trying to achieve? If not, what adaptations will be required? For what should each person on the team be responsible? Does the team have the right mix of behaviors? Are there any inherent blind spots that the team has as a result of their behavioral makeup? How will the team manage these blind spots?

One of my global clients often hires me to facilitate team meetings where we dig into the behavioral makeup of the team. We look at the Predictive Index® profiles of the individuals on the team. We discuss what the team is trying to accomplish and dig into potential issues that the team might face as a result of its members' Predictive Index® profiles. It starts with self-awareness. Each team member gets deep insights into their preferences, tendencies, drives, needs, and behaviors. Next, we discuss the collective makeup of the team. Finally, we go into the requirements of the team, sometimes discussing the implications associated with it working with other departments or specific clients.

Getting the information out on the table in an objective, data-driven way allows for candid discussion and a higher level of awareness. This process vastly reduces the amount of time it takes for a team to come together. Individuals develop their understanding of what makes each person tick. This method also enables team members to feel more confident to interact candidly, with a higher level of trust. They are less focused on guessing at how to communicate or manage interpersonal issues.

Fit with the Organization or Culture

The final fit to consider is the individual's fit to the overall organization or company culture. This last consideration has some overlap with core values discussed earlier, but with behavior, every company has a different feel. We often discuss this by considering the phase of the business cycle. Is the organization a start-up, a growth business, or in a state of maturity?

A start-up will require a lot more flexibility and agility than a mature business. Someone joining a start-up organization must be able to function well in a less structured environment. This situation often requires lower levels of formality and higher levels of dominance. However, there may still be individual roles, such as those in finance, that require a higher level of formality. Discussing the fit to the overall organization upfront will prepare new hires to integrate into the culture and understand some of the challenges they might experience there.

There are no hard and fast rules here, but in my experience, there are some tips to consider at each phase of the business cycle.

Start-Up Culture

I classify start-up organizations or business units as those that are just getting going. The business model is often unproven, or the organization is starting from ground zero. A start-up generally has a headcount of under 25 and definitely under 50. When working in a start-up or a very entrepreneurial venture, every employee must wear multiple hats. This culture requires flexibility and often people with lower levels of formality. People with high formality have a stronger need for rules and structures that often don't exist in a start-up environment. Start-ups additionally call for higher levels of dominance compared to the level of formality—a greater willingness to take risks and operate with uncertainty. Asking specific questions about how a candidate works in an unstructured environment can be very telling. Be sure to ask for real examples, not hypotheticals.

An additional factor I've observed in start-up ecosystems is lower levels of patience. These people generally enjoy variety in their work. They get bored and are less productive when doing routine activities. Working in a start-up frequently requires employees to do different types of work, often outside the specific tasks listed in their job description. People with high levels of patience will generally feel stressed with the constant change and lack of routine that is typical of most start-up environments. Again, ask for specific examples of how a candidate has operated in this type of environment in the past.

Growth Culture

I classify growth companies as those that have proven their business model and are at a point of reinvesting revenue generated from sales back into the organization for growth. The company may still be unprofitable, but the business model works, and it's now time to start establishing some systems and processes. In a growth business, there will generally be a shift from a high-risk, full-speed-ahead approach to one that features some risk and that moves fast—but with some consideration. Businesses in the growth phase generally have over 25 employees and are starting to form multiple layers of management, with individual managers responsible for overseeing the performance of their direct reports—a point at which it is incredibly important to establish a structured hiring process.

In a start-up, the CEO or founder of the business is typically involved in all hiring decisions. Once a company reaches about thirty-five to fifty employees, the founder should start delegating some of the hiring responsibilities to the department managers and individual team leads. Defined purpose, core values, and abilities related to a job's design are essential at this point. I see many fast-growing organizations falter at this stage. The quality of each additional hire starts to slip below what the founder would have considered appropriate.

At some point in the growth phase, a business will be required to start grouping roles by departments. Start by looking at customer-facing roles vs. back-office, non-customer-facing roles.

Customer-facing roles generally include those involved in sales, customer success, customer service, technical support, on-site

Chapter 6 – Abilities

delivery, and service.

Back-office, non-customer-facing roles include those involved in finance, design, development, operations, technology, analytics, and administration.

The first group generally requires higher levels of extroversion, as these people must enjoy interacting with people frequently.

The back-office, non-customer-facing roles often require lower levels of extroversion, as they have a greater focus on task work.

The team leads in each of these departments will also need to understand this and be comfortable working with, managing, and motivating employees who fit these profiles.

Mature Culture

I classify a mature business as one that has single- or low-double-digit growth in an industry that is well understood or has many established competitors. Mature companies can come in virtually any size. They can include franchise operations and financial-service practices, health care, and dental, etc., all the way up to large banks and multinational conglomerates. The key here is that the business is in a well-established space where things do not change rapidly. The focus is on keeping costs down while maintaining or improving efficiencies. These businesses generally have established processes and more levels of management. They will have well-understood managing relationships and metrics.

Overall, mature businesses will need higher levels of formality and patience at the operational level. They will require a mix of behaviors at the management and leadership level. One interesting observation I've made in recent years is that many mature businesses are getting displaced by new market entrants. If a business or industry is too focused on what's worked in the past, it runs the risk of getting displaced by new market entrants. Look at what happened to the taxicab industry when Uber entered.

To conclude, my advice for mature businesses is this: Match employees to roles that are well understood where the process is clearly defined. Keep investing in innovation and to encourage employees to take risks on new ideas, products, and services—as long as they fit with the overall business purpose defined in Chapter 4.

Identifying Top Performers

So, what exactly is a top performer? In some roles, like sales, the top-performer designation often goes to the rep with the highest sales numbers. You might also want to look at closing ratios or net promoter scores. No matter what the metric, the unknown has always been what makes each of the sales reps different. Data from assessments like the Predictive Index® allow organizations to quantify what makes each person unique in an objective and validated way.

Top-Performing Truck Drivers at Erb Group

Erb Group is a trucking and logistics company that specializes in refrigerated freight. They are the experts in temperature-controlled, time-sensitive food transportation. They operate over 1,000 trucks that make deliveries across Eastern Canada and the US.

I love working with larger companies like Erb because the number of employees in each position allows for some statistically significant analysis of what behaviors drive performance. During a driver-manager meeting early on in our relationship, we discussed how we planned to use the Predictive Index® to help with hiring. Predictive Index® has a strong history in the transportation and logistics industry. With over forty years of data from Canadian companies to draw on, we planned on using a profile from a previous study as a benchmark. At this meeting, one of the driver-managers was skeptical about the approach and mentioned that the Erb culture was unique in the trucking industry. He said they have many drivers who run rural routes, and the company already had an excellent safety record and low turnover rates. What if a great driver for Erb had a different profile from the companies we'd analyzed in the past?

This was an excellent opportunity to conduct a mini study to answer the following question: What makes for a great driver in the Erb culture? To get started, I asked the driver-managers to describe what they considered to be the characteristics of a great driver and a top performer. I stood at the front of the room and recorded their answers on the whiteboard.

The driver-managers mentioned the following qualities:
- friendly
- pleasant to work with
- willing to help and get the job done

- doesn't argue
- reliable
- polite
- punctual
- tidy
- customer-focused

I didn't limit their responses and didn't challenge them on anything. I didn't make this about Predictive Index® either. The goal here was to get the driver-managers to define what they believed made for a great driver for Erb, in their own words.

Once they had exhausted all their suggestions, I summarized their list. Next, I asked each of the driver-managers from the various terminals to think of five to seven drivers whom they believed embodied these characteristics. Then we had the driver-managers administer the Predictive Index® behavioral assessment to their selected five-to-seven top-performing drivers. I don't recall the exact numbers, but I believe we had forty or fifty driver profiles when all was said and done.

I created a group analysis for the company, looking at the group composite of what they considered to be their top drivers. The findings were astonishing. Not even one of the top drivers had a low level of formality. The overall group composite pattern suggested a very distinct pattern, too. The top drivers at Erb Group have a very high level of formality, a high level of patience, and a low level of extroversion. This finding was congruent with past studies we'd performed on profiles of top truck drivers. This comparative data was a great way to help make this real for the driver-managers who were going to start using this tool to help with hiring and driver management.

However, we were careful to caution them that the results didn't mean a driver who did not fit this profile couldn't do this job; it meant that they should be more careful with their interview and analysis. By using the data to facilitate the discussion, the driver-managers could ensure that the people they hired were right for the job and right for the culture at Erb.

What Is the Profile of a CEO?
An Analysis of the CEO of 1974 vs. the CEO of 2016

In 2016, we came across an article written by the founder of Predictive Index®, Arnold S. Daniels, in 1974. The report detailed a study he had conducted of 205 CEOs, vice presidents, presidents, and board chairpeople from 46 medium-to-large companies in the United States, Canada, and England. All of the profiles included in the study were from self-made business executives, 93 percent of whom achieved their positions in public companies. The others were entrepreneurs who had started or developed their own businesses. None of the executives was given their status through family ownership.

There were no specific performance metrics provided, but the article noted that the executives were rated highly by their peers as above average to exceptional. Arnold describes the pattern as an image of both experience and reality. The most exciting part of the analysis was the specificity and clarity with which the composite pattern described the required behaviors.

The composite pattern showed several very distinct factors. Note that I reference the sigma scale to indicate the degree of intensity of the factor. One sigma is equal to one standard deviation.

The dominance drive is very high, approximately 2.5 sigma to the right of the average, indicating a very strong need for impact and individual achievement. These executives will be conflict-tolerant and very assertive in their approach. Ninety-one percent of the executives assessed had high dominance profiles.

The patience drive is very low—approximately 2.5 sigma—indicating a very strong need for low patience and a very action-oriented approach. Ninety-six percent of the executives analyzed had low patience profiles.

While less extreme, both the extroversion and formality drives provided additional readings.

The formality drive is approximately 4/5th of a sigma low, indicating a need for some flexibility and adaptability. Eighty percent of the executives analyzed had a low level of formality.

The extraversion drive is approximately 1 sigma high, indicating a moderate-to-strong need for social interaction. Sixty-nine percent of the executives analyzed had a high level of extraversion.

These findings are the most useful when considering the demands of the position for selection and the development of future business executives. If an executive is found to have the required traits early in

Chapter 6 – Abilities

his or her career, he or she can be groomed to take on progressively more senior responsibilities.

In 2016, the customer success team at Predictive Success conducted a follow-up study of 173 CEOs of Canadian and American organizations to compare the results over time.

We observed similar results in this study; however, the resulting pattern was not as extreme. This new result indicates a need for a more adaptable CEO with slightly less intense behavior.

The result for each of the four primary drives follows. The dominance drive is high—approximately 1 sigma—indicating a moderate-to-strong need for impact and individual achievement. Eighty-six percent of the executives analyzed had a high level of dominance.

While still similar to 1974, this indicates that the CEO of 2016 is required to be slightly more team-oriented and less confrontational than his or her predecessor.

The patience drive is low—approximately 1 and 1/5th sigma—indicating a strong need for low patience and an action-oriented approach. Ninety-one percent of the executives analyzed had a low level of patience.

As in 1974, the patience drive is observed to be the most extreme factor; however, its level is less extreme in 2016, indicating a slightly calmer, more patient individual.

The extraversion drive displayed a wide distribution ranging from −3 sigma to +3 sigma. The average was very moderate, with a slight reading to the high side of 1/5th of a sigma. This result indicates a need for social adaptability.

The formality drive is displayed in over a narrow distribution, and the composite results fell on the average. This result indicates that the CEO of 2016 will require a moderate—not extraordinarily high or low—level of flexibility concerning rules orientation.

About the CEO Study

This CEO study focused on the composite synthesis pattern of the Predictive Index®. The synthesis pattern is a combination of the results from the self and self-concept patterns. This measure provides a combined analysis of the individual's native drives from the self-pattern and the individual's adaptive behaviors from the self-concept pattern. By looking at the composite synthesis of a large sample, we get a strong indication of the behaviors required for the CEO position. This type of study is a great way to quantify how the demands of jobs change over time and ensure the current benchmarks reflect the current behaviors of top performers.

Assessing General Cognitive Ability

The second part of the Predictive Index® assessment is a 12-minute timed cognitive ability assessment. The Predictive Index® Cognitive Assessment measures an individual's capacity to "learn quickly, grasp new concepts, adapt to changing circumstances, and understand complexity in the workplace. Cognitive ability is considered to be one of the best predictors of training success and job performance."[14]

How Does the Predictive Index® Cognitive Assessment Work?

The Predictive Index® Cognitive Assessment is administered online or via a computer terminal at an office. Assessment takers have 12 minutes to complete as many correct answers as possible to a set of fifty questions of varying difficulty. The assessment uses a mix of verbal, numerical, and abstract questions.

The test system uses a dynamic, test-building algorithm that ensures no two tests are the same. This feature minimizes the chances of cheating or gaining an advantage, should the candidate take the assessment more than once. The individual's score is compared to a target score for a given role or job function. Target scores are set using a job-targeting assessment or by compiling the scores of past successful incumbents. Scores at or above the target score indicate a strong probability of a candidate's ability to learn at an appropriate rate for the job. Scores below the target indicate that the candidate may have difficulties getting up to speed quickly enough for a given role. Again, these data are best used as part of a structured recruiting process to provide additional, objective data on the candidate.*

Always be sure to consult legal counsel when making decisions about assessment systems and processes for your company. Rules and regulations often differ by country and region. This book, in no way, intends to provide legal advice.

Chapter 6 – Abilities

Weighing Cognitive Data

One of the questions I often get is about how much weight to put in the cognitive-assessment results. My recommendation is to always apply a consistent approach for all candidates in a given role. This consistency helps reduce bias in the recruiting process. When determining how to use this data, there are a few things to consider.

How much ongoing learning is required in the role? If the position is well understood, and the amount of new learning is limited, the level of cognitive ability may not be very important. As mentioned earlier, I do a great deal of work with transportation organizations. Historically, the role of the truck driver has not changed much—thus, the level of cognitive ability was not weighted as heavily in the recruiting process.

My recommendation when hiring new graduates or people very early in their professional careers is to weigh cognitive ability a bit higher. When hiring someone with experience and specialized knowledge in an industry or job function, you may reduce the weighting. Ask yourself the following question: Am I hiring this person for the knowledge, experience, and skills they bring to my company, or am I expecting this person to learn on the job? If the latter, you are effectively investing in the person and paying for them to learn, which means you should consider weighing the cognitive abilities more heavily.

Get the cognitive score before you hire. There is no substitute for the pressure of a job interview and a timed assessment taken as part of an interview process. When clients attempt to administer the cognitive assessment to employees after they are hired, my experience has been that we get sub-optimal results. I hypothesize that the employee doesn't take the test as seriously, or perhaps the level of focus is not as high. Either way, I suggest making it part of the recruiting process and getting the assessment completed before hiring.

Interviewing with Assessment Data

Contrary to what you might be thinking at this point, using these assessments does not replace the need to conduct a structured interview. The assessment data enable you to focus your discussion on the candidate's strengths and potential weaknesses.

As we have discussed, there are specific abilities required for particular jobs. There are also nice-to-have abilities that will increase a candidate's (or an employee's) proficiency level.

Identifying the "non-negotiable" requirements is the first step to effectively assessing candidates and employees. If I am hiring a sales rep, an ability to effectively persuade and influence is going to be critical to the job. If I am hiring a bookkeeper, attention to detail is going to be necessary. Once I have identified the non-negotiables, the next step is to develop some behavior-based interview questions to probe for the candidates' past performance in this area.

When assessing for abilities, it is critical that you focus your questions on specific, real situations in which the candidate demonstrated their ability. Do not fall into the trap of asking hypothetical questions such as "What would you do if X . . . ?" or "How would you approach Y?" Instead, ask questions that start with tangible example lead-ins, such as "Give me an example of a time when X . . ." or "Tell me about a situation when you demonstrated your ability to do Y." There are many ways to conduct structured interviews. I often recommend the STAR method, where candidates are asked to describe a situation or task, provide the action they took, and describe the result they achieved.

ST – Situation or Task
A – Action
R – Result

It's fine to ask the candidate for real examples, and you might even explain that you expect them to tell you their past accomplishments. Remember, when it comes to hiring, past performance is the most significant predictor of future performance. If a candidate has done it before, you know they can do it again. Don't count on candidates who can miraculously change their approach or develop new abilities once you hire them—it can happen, but that's the exception to the rule.

 Talent Optimizer Tip: Use the STAR interview method. Ask candidates to recount a situation(s) or task(t), what

Chapter 6 – Abilities

> action(a) did they take, and what was the result(r) achieved?

Sample Interview Questions for the Four Behavioral Drives

Dominance Interview Questions

Examples of Questions for a Job that Requires High Dominance

When assessing for dominance, your goal is to investigate how the candidate impacts their environment. What results has the candidate been responsible for and what specific steps did they take to achieve them?

- Tell me about a time when you had to make an unpopular decision at work. How did you handle it with your team, employees, or staff? How did you get your team onside, and what was the outcome?
- Describe a situation in which you were responsible for initiating something new. What was the situation, and what was the result? How did you measure the success of the initiative?

Examples of Questions for a Job that Requires Low Dominance

When assessing for low dominance, your goal is to determine how the candidate cooperates and seeks harmony in the workplace. You are looking for examples of how they support their team or peers and take an unselfish approach to work.

- Tell me about a time when you had to take on a support role and let others set the direction. How did you support the team? What were you responsible for? How did your actions help the team achieve results?
- Describe a situation in which you helped to resolve a conflict. What was the issue? What actions did you take to defuse the situation?

Extraversion Interview Questions

Examples of Questions for a Job that Requires High Extraversion

When assessing for high extraversion, your goal is to determine how the candidate approaches social interaction. Look for examples of how they built relationships and worked in a social environment.

- Tell me about a time when you had to solve a complex project while working closely with many other people.
- Describe a situation in which you were responsible for changing the opinions of others. What was the situation? How did you win people over?

Examples of Questions for a Job that Requires Low Extraversion

When assessing for low extraversion, your goal is to determine how the candidate approaches individual task-oriented work.

- Tell me about a time when you had to solve a complex project while working exclusively on your own.
- Describe a situation that demonstrates your analytical ability.

Patience Interview Questions

Examples of Questions for a Job that Requires High Patience

When assessing for high patience, your goal is to determine how the candidate approaches repetitive and routine work. Look for examples of how they operate in a stable environment.

- Tell me about a time when you were required to perform a repetitive task. What did you like or dislike about it?
- Describe a situation that required you to focus on one project for a long period of time and to stick with it through to completion. How long did it take? What setbacks did you persist through?

Examples of Questions for a Job that Requires Low Patience

When assessing for low patience, your goal is to determine how the candidate approaches fast-paced work with frequent changes. Look for examples of how they operate in a changing environment.

- Tell me about a time when you had to deal with many competing priorities or projects. How did you prioritize things?
- Describe a situation in which you had to complete a project under an extremely tight deadline. How did you deal with the time pressure? How did the time pressure affect you?

Formality Interview Questions

Examples of Questions for a Job that Requires High Formality

When assessing for high formality, your goal is to determine how the candidate approaches rules and structure. Look for examples of how the candidate operates in a structured environment.

- Tell me about a time when you were required to follow a plan exactly as directed.
- Describe a system you use to keep yourself organized.

Examples of Questions for a Job that Requires Low Formality

When assessing for low formality, your goal is to determine the candidate's flexibility with respect to rules and structure. Look for examples of how the candidate was able to find creative solutions.

- Tell me about a time when you were required to be flexible with your approach to problem-solving.
- Describe a situation in which you were required to make a decision that involved incomplete information or a lot of uncertainty.

Chapter 6 Summary

Defining the abilities of a role is a critical step to ensuring you have the right people in the right seats. The use of assessments can greatly increase your effectiveness at this step in the Talent Optimizer process. The assessments should be used as a guide to help you identify possible red flags or opportunities. By assessing your current team, you will gain valuable insights into what each person needs to thrive and do their best work. The first step here is always self-discovery; you must first understand your own drives, needs, and behaviors. Once you have a good understanding of how the behavioral model works, you can start to hire and inspire others more effectively.

Chapter 6 Action Steps

1. Add a validated assessment solution like the Predictive Index® to your recruiting and succession process.
2. Develop job targets for all roles before beginning your next recruiting project.
3. Use the assessments to help guide your interview process.
4. For each interview, create a list of structured questions to ask all candidates. As you get answers to these questions from multiple candidates, you will build your mental model for what good answers sound like.
5. Review your successful and unsuccessful hires against the job targets at least annually. Track your results to determine the behavioral and cognitive factors impacting success or failure.

CHAPTER 7 – SKILLS

Skills Come Last?

First, we address values, then abilities, and then skills. We do it in this order for a reason. If the values don't match, the candidate should be eliminated because nothing else matters, they are not right for your company culture. If hired, the resulting negative effect on the overall workplace culture will far outweigh any positives from the skills. We address abilities second, as there may be a variety of places to use a great person with a set of abilities in an organization. Also, when implemented effectively, this talent-optimizer process often identifies lateral moves and succession opportunities that may have otherwise gone overlooked. My mantra here is: if we get great people who believe in a shared set of values, we will always have a place for them as the company grows. It's also important to remember that abilities are difficult to change but not impossible. If someone is highly motivated to adapt their approach, they may be able to sustain it for a period of time.

Technology and Skills

Technology is changing the way business is done at a faster rate every year. I've long given talks at universities and trade associations on the pace of change and how technology has impacted the workplace over the past several hundred years. As referenced in the prologue, the businessman originally invested in hired hands. Then, just before the turn of the nineteenth century, the development of water and steam power and the mechanical production factory came, and this changed the type of skills needed in the workplace.

It took nearly 100 years for the next significant leap. In 1879, Edison invented the lightbulb, paving the way for extended factory hours, and then came Henry Ford's production line in 1913. By specializing in one area, the division of labor allowed for greater levels of productivity and production per capita. These innovations dramatically shifted the skills required, displaced some jobs, and created some new jobs. The production supervisor now had to oversee the performance and productivity of many workers.

The next significant innovation took roughly another 100 years. Richard E. Morley founded Bedford Associates and, in 1969, invented the first programmable logic controller, or PLC, the Modicon 084. These automated production machines eliminated another class of workers but created a new set of jobs requiring a new set of skills, shifting manual-labor roles to knowledge-worker roles again. The next revolution took only about 40 years, as today we have the internet of things and connected cyber-physical systems.

My point with all of this is simple: The rate of technological innovation is increasing. The days in which a person could become a craftsman and be assured job security for a lifetime are behind us.

In his book *Sapiens*, Yuval Noah Harari explores the impact of technology on society and the human race. The average lifespan of a human is increasing. By his estimates, a baby born today may have a life expectancy of greater than a hundred years, with the potential of living beyond 150 with the help of biotechnology and nanotechnology. Think about the impact this would have on the working class. Skills become obsolete every fifteen or twenty years, and a working adult may need to re-skill three or four times in a working lifetime. In our lifetime, we have seen massive changes in low-skilled roles. Every year, more and more jobs are replaced by automation. The barriers to outsourcing via online freelance have been virtually eliminated.

Because skills can be learned and often need to be upgraded, I recommend doing this part last. If you get the first steps right, you may find that you can train the skills.

Chapter 7 – Skills

 Talent Optimizer Tip: Assess for skills last. If you find great people you can teach them new skills.

In some situations where you are under the gun for a specific skill set to solve an immediate problem, you might need to hire for skills first, but those situations should be the exception to the rule and treated with caution and a very clearly defined plan.

Assessing for Skills by Role

In my experience, there is no substitute for a real-life situation, so try to give real challenges or work to candidates whenever possible. The examples that follow are some of the more common roles that require specialized skills.

Computer Science

Consider creating a coding challenge or problem set for the candidate to solve. Be sure to watch how they approach the problem to evaluate their problem-solving approach.

Administration

Give the candidate a real-life example of what they will be doing. Have them respond to sample e-mails. Test for grammar, clarity of communication, and detail orientation. Consider doing a typing test to measure words per minute.

Marketing & Creative

If hiring for a marketing role, give the candidate a hypothetical marketing assignment. For example, say, "We are an online jewelry company interested in expanding into a new market segment. Create a marketing plan including your suggestions and the metrics you would use to measure the success of your program."

Talent Optimizer Tip: Consider giving the candidate the assignment on short notice or on a Friday afternoon with a deadline of nine o'clock Monday morning. This is a great way to see how much the candidate wants the job. Are they willing to give up a weekend for a shot at landing it?

Sales

When hiring for a sales role, there is no substitute in having the candidate sell you something. My recommendation here is to have the candidate sell you something they know well, like a product or service with which they have experience. I often see companies ask candidates to sell the company's products or services. In my experience, this is a mistake. At this stage of the interview, you are assessing for existing sales and presentation skills. By asking the candidate to memorize the product features on the spot, you are complicating the process and will not be able to truly evaluate their true sales proficiency. I would rather have a candidate sell me something they know inside and out, so they can focus on their questions and information-gathering as opposed to presenting unfamiliar features and benefits.

 Talent Optimizer Tip: Do not ask sales candidates to present your products or services at the interview stage. Instead, ask the candidate to sell you something they have sold before, or something with which they are familiar.

General and Unskilled Labor

For general laborer roles, consider hiring the candidate on a trial basis to evaluate their skills and proficiency.

Production Management

Give the candidates a case study with real examples. Have them build you a production schedule with real orders and real employee data. Ask them to walk you through their thinking and approach.

Chapter 7 – Skills

You are looking for a good approach and sound logic. Don't get hung up if a candidate doesn't follow your exact system.

Project Management

Ask the candidates to demonstrate their project management approach. Are they trained in a specific system? Do they use agile methodology? Have the candidates walk you through a sample sprint.

Finance

If you are hiring an accountant or finance person, be sure to administer a live test of his or her computer and Excel skills. I made the mistake of not doing so early in my career when I hired a CFO who had a ton of experience with accounting principles but was virtually computer illiterate. He typed with two fingers, and it took him hours to do simple accounting tasks that should have taken only a few minutes.

Management Roles

Ask the candidate to role-play a one-on-one feedback or coaching session with you that demonstrates his or her management skills inside a dictated scenario.

> Talent Optimizer Tip: The best person to assess for skills is the top performer currently doing the job or the manager who will be overseeing the role. If no one at the company has expertise in the area you are hiring, then you should leverage your network to find someone to assist

Final Thought

The skills assessment is an important part of the recruitment process. If you haven't done a good job here in the past or don't know where to start, consider leveraging your existing team's expertise. The next time a manager asks for an additional team member, make the manager develop a skills assessment along with an evaluation process before approving the hire. Over time, you will build a library of skills assessments by role.

Chapter 7 – Skills

Chapter 7 Action Steps

The action steps will be different for each job. The key takeaway here is to make the skills assessment as objective as possible and to include someone you trust who has a high level of proficiency in the area being assessed to evaluate the skills in question. Create a scoring rubric to help you evaluate the skills proficiency.

CHAPTER 8 – DESIRE AND WORK VALUES

"Our potential is one thing. What we do with it is quite another."
— Angela Duckworth[15]

Once purpose, values, abilities, and skills are aligned, the final thing to assess for is desire and what I will call work values.

At this point in the hiring process, you should have the right person (work values) with the right abilities (behavior and cognitive ability) with the right skills or ability to acquire the right skills in short order. So, we should have all the stars aligned, right? No, unfortunately, we are not done yet.

Grit, Spunk, Determination, Chutzpah, Drive, or Desire

Some people call it *grit* or *drive*. I like to call it *desire*. Does the person in question have the desire to do the job in question? Desire can't be forced. If someone doesn't want to do a job or believes the job is beneath him/her, there's no amount of leadership training or team-building that will change this—the person simply isn't going to be a good fit for the role.

In his book, *Traction*, Gino Wickman describes this part as *GWC*. Does the person "get it"? Do they understand the job and what needs to be done? Do they "want it" or have the desire to do the job? Does the person have the "capacity" to do the job?

Chapter 8 – Desire and Work Values

G = Gets it
W = Wants it
C = Capacity to do it

Before you hire someone, you should ensure you have three checkmarks here.

Interviewing for Desire

Desire can be difficult to identify at the interview stage. When candidates are at an interview, they are not likely to come out and say they think the job is beneath them, especially if they are early in their career or unemployed. Luckily, I have come across some good ideas for desire-related interview questions.

Dev Basu, whom you met in Chapter 5, asks candidates to describe an activity or task they used to do that they no longer like doing. This is a great way to get a candidate talking about the type of things they feel they have outgrown or progressed beyond. If a sales rep is applying for an outside sales role and mentions that they used to have to spend a lot of time cold-calling but no longer like doing it, that's a great indication that they might not be right for the job.

Additional Desire Questions

Thinking about your last job, what were your most important responsibilities? What aspects did you like best and least?

Every job has its ups and downs. Thinking about your last job, tell me about the things you really looked forward to doing most. Follow up: What do you least like doing?

Work Values

In the book *The Leadership Pipeline*, the authors Ram Charan, Stephen Drotter, and James Noel describe work values as the type of work the executive values and deems to be important. When an executive progresses through a career, each successive promotion requires an increase in management and leadership activities paired with a decrease in individual contributor activities.

For example, if an accountant is hired as a bookkeeper, the first several years of that employee's career might involve working on spreadsheets, generating proformas, and doing actual accounting work. If, after a period of time, the worker displays excellent proficiency, the company might offer a promotion to an accounting manager role. If the employee agrees to take on this role, he or she must start to delegate work to subordinates. Further, he or she must make time to provide coaching and guidance to his or her direct reports, and he or she must begin to value these manager activities as more important than the individual contributor activities he or she was responsible for previously. They must now give up the personal satisfaction they once enjoyed from crossing tasks off a to-do list and begin to find it in getting results through others. This is a fundamental shift in employee responsibilities, and it takes a change of mindset.

 Talent Optimizer Key Point: Becoming a manager of others requires that one recognize that the greatest use of one's time is no longer getting things done as efficiently and effectively as possible but creating an environment in which others can get things done as efficiently and effectively as possible.

The Leadership Pipeline explores this concept in great detail and provides a guide for leaders as they transition through the six leadership transition points.

Leadership Transitions

- Passage 1: From leader of self to leading others
- Passage 2: From leading others to leading leaders
- Passage 3: From leading leaders to functional leader
- Passage 4: From functional leader to business leader
- Passage 5: From business leaders to group leader
- Passage 6: From group leader to enterprise leader.

The Leadership Pipeline Institute[16] has created a leadership development program designed to help leaders make each transition. In the intensive four-day training program, leaders are educated on the expectations and trained on the skills required at each level. As part of my work with Predictive Success, I had the opportunity to attend the program with a client in Chicago. The course provides managers with the foundational knowledge required to be an effective leader.

Assessing for Work Values

I have two lines of questioning for assessing work values at the interview stage.

First, you must identify the passage level at which the candidate should be operating. If using the passage structure from *The Leadership Pipeline*, you might consider making a list of expectations for what an executive should value at each stage. For a detailed list, I suggest you read *The Leadership Pipeline*.

For example, let's use the "Leading Others" level. A manager at this level should value getting results through others, be proficient at training and onboarding new employees, and understand and value giving feedback to their reports.

For candidates applying for a leadership position who come from a similar-level role at another organization, ask them to imagine they are at their last job and that their manager at an annual review asks them to describe the three things they did in the past year to deserve a raise or a bonus.

Have the candidate describe in detail what they did and the results they achieved.

What you are looking for here is the level of the activities they described. Were they individual contributor activities that are required at the leadership level that the candidate is applying for? This is a very telling exercise, and it will help you determine if the candidate values the right activities and outcomes for their job level.

Follow-up Questions

How was your performance measured in your last role? (If it was not measured, ask the candidate how they would measure their performance and to provide examples of what they did.)

Give me a detailed breakdown of the most important weekly meetings and tasks you performed in your last role to ensure you would accomplish your goals.

Describe the initiatives you implemented to increase the overall productivity of your team. (Probe for specifics. Make notes to ask references about this later.)

Chapter 8 Action Steps

1. Add Desire questions to your interview process.
2. Map your organizational chart and note at which level each role should be operating.
3. Add work-values questions to your interview process.

CHAPTER 9 – SOURCING TALENT

Magnetically Attract Talent with a Custom Job Posting

It always amazes me how few companies take the time to create a custom job posting for every role. Then, they are surprised when they get average or below-average applicants.

Think about the job posting as your first impression on the candidate. Don't you want the candidate reading the job posting to feel like it was written just for them?

The Three-Part Job Posting

For each job posting, you should include the following three parts.

Person Description

This part should describe the characteristics of the ideal person for this role. The goal here is to be clear and polarizing. Make it very obvious what abilities you are looking for; be direct, and be blunt. See the sales example below.

Company Description

Your company description is the first thing a potential applicant will see when they begin their application process with your company.

The company description should provide a summary of what makes the company and culture unique.

This is where you will include your core values and purpose. Some companies will lead with their core values and purpose.

Opportunity Description

The opportunity description describes the position in more detail. Be sure to include how this position will be evaluated and any relevant information the candidate might need to know about the role, such as:

- Location—on-site or remote
- Work hours and travel, if applicable
- Key responsibilities
- Desired competencies
- Required or desired knowledge, skills, experience
- Additional requirements

Customize Your Descriptions

The best descriptions include language that will appeal to the type of candidate you seek.

Use this list of adjectives to help populate your job posting to attract your ideal candidate magnetically. Be sure to pull adjectives from the factors that you believe are most critical to the success of the role.

Talent Optimizer

	Extremely Low	Very Low	Moderately Low	Moderately High	Very High	Extremely High
Dominance	Service-oriented Selfless	Collegial Team-oriented Generous	Unselfish Cooperative Sharing Giving	Confident Independent Competitive Self-starter	Assertive Resourceful Innovative	Aggressive Forceful Controlling
Extraversion	Private Introspective	Thoughtful Imaginative Reflective Task-oriented	Reserved Serious Analytical	Persuasive Social Fluent Talkative	Socially-poised Extroverted Stimulating Enthusiastic	Gregarious Cheerful
Patience	Extremely fast Pressure-seeking	Intense Driving Action oriented Results focused	Fast paced Impatient with routine	Relaxed Calm Stable Methodical Patient	Systematic Deliberate Unhurried Step-by-step Routine	Habitual Sequential
Formality	Extremely flexible Uninhibited Non-conforming	Innovative Adaptable Risk tolerant Generalist	Independent Informal Flexible Uninhibited	Accurate Careful Thorough Disciplined	Precise Cautious Exacting Expert Dutiful Risk-averse	Perfectionist Specific By-the-book Specialist Conforming

Table 9-1

Chapter 9 – Sourcing Talent

Superstar Sales Hire

Below is part of an article I wrote for a LinkedIn post aimed at helping clients find superstar salespeople.

The problem most organizations have when hiring top sales talent is that they don't know how to attract it or evaluate it.

The first step in attracting top sales talent is determining what you require. Here, I am going to focus on how to hire a sales hunter.

A hunter salesperson has a distinct behavioral profile. We see this frequently in our validity studies across a wide variety of industries. There are three key factors and one secondary factor one needs to look for in sales.

The Superstar Sales Hunter

High Dominance: Your salesperson must have a high drive for control and a desire to win.

High Extroversion: Your salesperson needs to be able to build relationships and connect socially with prospects.

Low Patience: The best salespeople move fast. They can manage multiple opportunities at the same time. They enjoy working in a fast-paced environment.

The most critical combination of the above factors is High Dominance with Low Patience—a very proactive style.

There is an essential secondary factor, which is the dark horse that makes a huge difference: *empathy*. Without empathy, you run the risk of hiring a jerk with confidence, who may perform but will leave a path of destruction in his or her wake.

Confident, persuasive people with the right amount of empathy will put clients' needs first and, by persuading them like crazy, help them make the right decision.

Now that we know what we are looking for, the next step is to craft a job posting that will attract the type of person who fits that profile and repel those who don't.

The Superstar Sales Hunter Job Posting

I recently worked with a client in transportation to create this job posting.[17]

Looking for Top Performers $80k - $300k+

Don't even apply unless you are an **overachiever** and can **prove it**. We are a Toronto-based transportation company seeking a few **superstar salespeople** to help us **achieve** our **aggressive growth** targets of 18% per year over the next five years.

We invest in our people and **pay generously**: earn $80k if you are average, **earn $300k+** if you are a **superstar, we do NOT cap earnings**. Our people enjoy a clean, modern, and technology-enabled workplace. We **empower** our people to **take action**, and our sales reps enjoy a high level of **autonomy** and **flexibility**.

We are a leading transportation industry innovator; we are small enough to act with **agility** and large enough to service top national brands.

We are looking for cross-border sales, but we don't hire experience or backgrounds—we **hire top producers**. Young or old, if you have the stuff, we'll know it.

To apply, please complete a Predictive Index® survey using the link below and email your resume to the address below.

Notice that we didn't include anything about the company history or required experience. The focus here is to call out top performers. The funny thing about top performers is that they find a way to rise to the top in everything they do. I've hired sales reps with no industry experience who quickly outperformed veteran employees.

Notice the terms in bold. I've chosen specific adjectives to appeal to the type of person who fits our ideal candidate profile. This strategy works for all types of positions—by starting with the behavioral profile of the ideal candidate, you can easily craft a job posting that will compel them to respond. I often work with clients to help perfect this language, and it has a considerable impact on applicant quality.

Handwritten Social Media Job Posting

For another strategy, try writing out the posting on a piece of paper, snap a photo, and post it on your LinkedIn. Here's an example of what this looks like from a recent client in Telecom:

Chapter 9 – Sourcing Talent

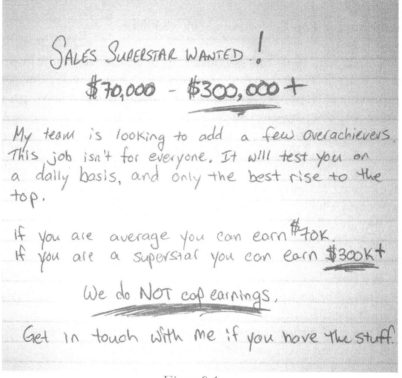

Figure 9-1

Another essential tip for attracting top sales talent is to list the right earning potential. I often see companies listing the average earnings for a salesperson in their job postings. This makes absolutely zero sense. If you are looking for superstar salespeople, state the absolute most anyone has ever made in this role. If you post average earning potential, you will get average-quality candidates; if you post exceptional earning potential, you will get exceptional candidates. I recently sat in on an interview and asked the candidate why this job posting appealed to her. She answered candidly, "I like that you had a + sign next to the salary."

 Talent Optimizer Tip: Do not list average earnings in job postings for sales talent. List the maximum earning potential for the role, or the most anyone has ever earned in the role.

Driver-Manager Job Posting

Here is another example of a job posting for a driver-manager or dispatch role we created for one of my trucking clients. Note that I've removed the company description.

Driver-Manager/Dispatcher Wanted!
We are looking for a **master multi-tasker** with **excellent communication skills** and an **upbeat, positive attitude.** Candidates will need to manage the day-to-day communication with drivers and be the bridge between our operations department and the field staff.

To be successful as a driver-manager, candidates should be **professional, polite,** and **calm under pressure** while also being **accurate.** They should always be thinking two steps ahead and willing to **meet each challenge directly.** Driver-managers must be comfortable with computers and general office tasks and should excel at both verbal and written communication. Most importantly, the driver-manager should have a genuine interest in **working with people, solving problems,** and **effectively communicating** directions.

Driver-Manager Responsibilities:
The driver-manager is responsible for working with an assigned group of drivers to ensure effective communication and distribution of scheduled assignments. This role involves dispatch duties, following driver movements, and proactively managing hours of service. This position works closely with the dispatch planner to ensure that delivery schedules and customer expectations are met while maximizing equipment utilization.

As the key contact person, the driver-manager is the face of the organization to many of our most valued employees. Building a positive working relationship with drivers is required to achieve both driver retention and customer-service goals.

The ideal candidate will have at least one year of transportation-related industry experience or a college/related industry certificate.

Driver-Manager Requirements:
- Excellent communication skills, both verbal and written,

especially typing. Multilingual preferred but not required.
- Ability to remain calm and work effectively in a fast-paced environment with frequent tight deadlines.
- Excellent attention to detail.
- Ability to solve problems effectively and communicate solutions calmly to drivers, internal stakeholders, and customers.

A Strategic Approach to Truck-Driver Recruitment

Some say trucking is the lifeblood of the US economy. Nearly 71% of all the freight tonnage moved in the States goes on trucks, so it's safe to say the trucking industry is necessary to keep the American economy functioning. There is a driver shortage crisis.

The American Trucking Association (ATA) estimates that there are 3.6 million trucks and 3.5 million truck drivers in the United States. As of 2018, the ATA estimates a shortage of 60,000 drivers, which is expected to grow to 174,000 by 2026.[18] The industry is experiencing something of a perfect storm. The average age of the current driver workforce is fifty-five, nearly ten years older than that of workers in other comparable blue-collar jobs, like manufacturing.[19] As these drivers retire, the industry isn't seeing new entrants come in to replace them. The industry is nearly 95% male-dominated, and the immigration laws in Canada and the United States are adding pressure to the situation as driving is not recognized as a skilled profession. (As an aside, I find this ridiculous as I can't imagine an unskilled driver backing an eighteen-wheeler into a loading dock between two other trucks, but that's a debate I'll save for another time.) Suffice to say, sourcing quality drivers is becoming incredibly tricky in both Canada and the United States.

Imagine for a moment that you are the owner of a trucking company and have an opportunity to make a recruiting presentation to a stadium filled with 50,000 of your ideal drivers. These are the excellent drivers—they don't speed; they obey traffic laws; they keep accurate logs. They also fit with your company culture and have the right behavioral profile to do the job. Oh, and they have experience driving the type of routes for which you are looking to hire them. However, in this stadium, 99% of the drivers are already employed at another trucking company.

Only about 1% of them are in transition and interested in making a move to a new company.

That means 33% of the drivers are *not thinking about* making a change but might be open to it if you made a persuasive pitch.

It means 33% of the drivers *think* they are not interested in making a change. They believe they are already at the best company or that it's not worth changing.

And it means 33% of the drivers *know* they are not interested in making a change—maybe they work for a family business or are nearing retirement.

So, you are given the opportunity to go out on stage in front of this stadium filled with drivers in all four categories listed above and make a recruiting presentation. The only caveat is this—just before you walk out on stage, the drivers are advised that, while they had to show up, if what you have to say is not of interest, they can get up and leave.

The question becomes: What can you say you are going to talk about on that stage that will keep everyone in their seats?[20] Realize that you have people who "know they are not interested" in making a change.

Pioneered by the late Chet Holmes for use in sales and marketing, this concept is called a "stadium pitch." If you can answer the above question effectively, you have a good shot of capturing your ideal drivers' interest. So, what do you talk about? Well, the answer is not to get up on stage and talk about wages or work-life balance, or your company culture. In fact, you should not talk about anything at all related to your company. The trick is to use what is called "market data" to educate the drivers on what they should be looking for in a quality company. To teach them what they are missing out on in their current situation. Market data is paramount when you are mass marketing. Focus on what matters to the target and lead them to your unique value proposition.

Let's take a look at how Carmen Transportation, whom you met in Chapter 4, did this effectively. Carmen is growing, and they are always looking for additional drivers. As you can imagine, they aren't willing to hire just any driver. Every driver must fit with the company values, and they always assess for behavior and ability fit before extending an offer.

I sat down with the recruitment team several years ago to

brainstorm strategies for attracting quality drivers.

The first idea we came up with was to apply some internet marketing strategies to their offline marketing. Virtually every trucking company runs recruitment ads in the free magazines and booklets that you can pick up at gas stations and rest stops. The next time you are at a rest stop, have a look at these help-wanted ads, and you'll see that every single company says the same thing. They all offer benefits; they all offer competitive wages; they all claim to have the best fleet and the best trucks. The point is, no one was doing anything different to stand out.

I saw this as a great opportunity.

First, we listed all of the unique features that benefit drivers that Carmen offers and other companies don't. The goal here was not to *start* with the benefits but to make drivers aware of them and want them.

The team gave their ideas and I listed them on the whiteboard. By the end of our session, we had ten or twelve unique benefits to working with Carmen. We summarized these for use later.

Next, we realized that the drivers who are looking for jobs at truck stops are probably not the best in the industry. We also recognized that drivers who switch jobs for a cent or two per kilometer were not going to be worth investing in hiring. So, leading with a pay-per-kilometer offer was probably a mistake. The drivers we were looking to target were the best drivers at other companies. They were the drivers who were already earning a steady wage and were probably not thinking about making a switch.

Finally, we thought about who would be seeing the ad, and we tried to imagine their point of view. This driver probably picked up the magazine at a rest stop they'd stopped at to refuel or grab a bite to eat. So we had to think to ourselves: What could we say that would be of interest to every single driver who reads this? This group would include drivers who had just started with other companies; drivers who were happy with their current employers; drivers who were unhappy with their current employers—for the most part, drivers who weren't thinking about finding another opportunity.

After a lot of back and forth, we came up with the following ad.

WHAT DRIVERS DON'T KNOW!

The 5 SECRETS your trucking employer is keeping from you!

Discover what it costs you...

www.expectmoretrucking.com

Figure 9-2

Notice the ad doesn't mention the company name; it doesn't mention pay; it doesn't mention benefits. It just hooks the driver to learn more.

Think about the person(s) to whom this ad appeals. *Everyone.* Happy drivers, frustrated drivers, experienced drivers, new drivers. It doesn't matter—every driver will want to know what secrets their company might be keeping from them. I created the landing page on a separate website, or "micro-site," expectmoretrucking.com, as a way to capture leads. This site allows us to stay in touch with the drivers who were interested in learning more about the differences in working with a great company but weren't ready to apply yet.

If you visit www.expectmoretrucking.com, you will notice there is still no mention of Carmen until after you enter your contact info—the site only has a copy of the ad and a form to access the report.

The driver must enter their contact info to get the report. Sure, some people provide fake info, and that's always going to happen. Once they read the report, some percentage of those people will get in touch after.

Chapter 9 – Sourcing Talent

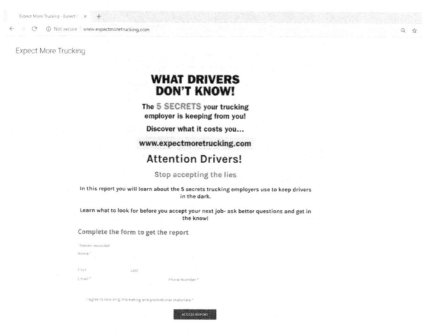

Figure 9-3

The report details five areas that create confusion in the way trucking companies download costs to drivers: things like not paying for border dwell times or paying by load volume as opposed to by distance. The most important part of the report is that it educates drivers about the differences between working for a driver-first company and the average company. If great drivers read the report, they might all of a sudden realize that their current company is not compensating them fairly. If this happens and the driver gets frustrated, they are more likely to reach out to Carmen as their next best option because Carmen educated them for free and didn't ask for anything in return. Carmen takes the approach of giving to drivers with no expectation of reciprocity. Advertising for drivers using market data is a strategic investment, and it pays off in the long run when quality drivers are ready to make a change. This strategy generated over 150 leads in the first year; the company's previous advertisements in the same magazine did not produce a single lead.

 Talent Optimizer Tip: Create your stadium pitch—what information will appeal to everyone in your target audience.

Talent Optimizer Tip: Create a different microsite or landing page for each ad. Microsites allow you to track your success rates and measure your results.

Social Media Recruiting

Next, I sat down with social media and digital advisor Sulemaan Ahmed. Sulemaan is a principal at Servo-annex. He and his partner founded the firm eight years ago.

"I've always worked in technology," he said. "I've got a business degree in commerce. I did a masters in computer science. I've worked for fairly big companies, e-commerce groups, organizations like Air Canada, Apple, Huffington Post. I reached a point where I decided I didn't want to work for big companies anymore. I wanted to look at working within the start-up space. Today, we specialize in teaching senior executives and the c-suite on how to use digital platforms, whether for sales, marketing, or recruitment. So, it is not just posting something up, but understanding how the post drives an outcome or a specific result from an ROI perspective."

Sulemaan and I discussed how executives use digital platforms to help with recruitment. He mentioned that several clients have a specific focus on hard-to-fill roles or extremely competitive industries like tech and computer science. The challenge most executives face is how to differentiate what they offer from the executive down the street. Today's job seekers want to know what's in it for them. If they have options, share why you expect them to work for you. "You can't leave it up to HR to generate a generic job posting and hope you get great people," Ahmed said. "It's not going to happen."

The executives who do a great job of this are taking a different approach to supplement the work HR and recruiting do on this front. He provided three suggestions.

First, you must figure out what platform your target employees are using. If it's banking or finance, it's probably LinkedIn. If it's media or government, it's most likely Twitter. If it's marketing or advertising, it might be Instagram or Facebook. This step boils down to fishing where the fish are.

Once you know the platform, step two is to professionalize your profile. Make sure your profile name is consistent with your business

Chapter 9 – Sourcing Talent

name. Ensure your headshot is consistent with the headshot potential candidates will see on the company directory. Complete your profile with all relevant information. Include your personal values, work philosophy, accomplishments, and awards. Sharing this information is an opportunity to brand yourself, so your target candidates will see you as a desirable boss. If you have been at the company for a while, have your direct reports write endorsements for you.

Once your profile is optimized, connect with all of your direct reports, peers, clients, suppliers, and other relevant business contacts. Using platforms like LinkedIn to get the word out about a new opportunity is a cost-effective way to bring in referrals and leverage your network.

Employer Branding and Career Sites

Phil Strazzulla is the founder and CEO of Nextwave Hire, a company specializing in employer branding and career sites. I interviewed Phil to get his thoughts on what makes for a great career site and what leading companies are doing to use culture to attract great people.

Phil describes himself as a lifelong entrepreneur. Phil got the idea for Nextwave Hire while attending Harvard Business School. He found his classmates continually talking about how hard it was to understand what it was like to work at any company. Like a true entrepreneur, he thought to himself: There's got to be a better way.

Phil explains that "most companies just kind of have job postings, and this was even truer back in 2013 and 2014. They didn't tell what it's like to work at the company. Glassdoor was only starting up at that point, and there was some content there, but it was even more negatively biased than it is today. The only people leaving reviews were people who got fired. You had to know somebody or go into the alumni directory and search for who used to work at XYZ Company to see if you could get an informational interview with them.

"I just thought that's crazy, especially since where you work is such an important decision in your life. So, I started a business to help companies share their culture through employee stories. We collect the stories through our software and show off what's it like to be an engineer at the company, what's it like to be in the New York office versus Vancouver versus wherever. That's kind of how the company started, and then it evolved from there to solve the problem for HR around how do we use culture to attract people effectively? That led to: How do we revamp the career website and how do we have more information on social media. Next, how do we take all those people who are not ready to apply yet and engage them over time through what we call 'talent communities'? That's the genesis of Nextwave."

Next, I asked Phil about the type of companies that most often use his services

Phil: "The majority of the companies we work with are fast-growing technology companies. I'd say that they are probably half of our customers. Then the other 50% are scattered across financial services, consumer goods, whatever. I think the commonality is that they're all looking to hire awesome people, and their HR teams are a little bit more forward-thinking. I think that is what is needed to do the new thing. We need to remember that our customers are not super tech-savvy. They've never run a website before; they don't know much about marketing. We're asking them to do all this stuff they've never done before, so we start really, really simple."

Phil: "Everything in our solution is designed to be up and running in a couple of minutes. We usually start with a talent community on the website, which takes about five minutes to set up and drives a lot of ROI. We now allow companies to start with that on a standalone basis. If they want to try the talent-community aspect of things, we update the career site. We collect a lot of content from the employees. We send out e-surveys and ask them the questions that they get asked from candidates, like: What do you do on a day-to-day basis? If it's an engineer: what's the tech stack? If it's a salesperson: Why do people buy the products?"

"We build out their employer brand, and then go back and measure everything so that we understand what is driving results. For example, say, we added micro-sites for the key functions within our company. How did that change the percentage of visitors to the career site who applied for a job? We added a talent community. How many people are we getting into that? How many hires are we making from that, etc.?"

Nextwave effectively took what internet marketing professionals have been doing for years and applied the concept to recruitment.

Chapter 9 – Sourcing Talent

Phil described the candidate experience: "So, the candidate journey starts when I find out about the company. Maybe somebody posted something on LinkedIn. I go to the career site. I check out the micro-site that's about people like me—maybe that's women in tech; maybe it's people in the Boston office—and I'm like, 'OK. This is a cool company. I'm not ready to apply—I don't have a resume. Maybe it's because I'm still in school. Maybe I just switched jobs three months ago. Whatever the case may be, I'm not ready to apply to the Applicant Tracking System (ATS).'

"What we do with the talent community is we say, 'OK. You don't have to apply to the ATS. Just leave your name and e-mail and what job you're interested in, and then every month, we'll keep you updated on what's going on with the company.' That, usually, is culture content, not so many job posts. It's more like, 'Hey, check out Nancy, who got promoted from Sales Development Rep (SDR) to Account Executive. Check out Mike's interview tips for engineering roles at our company. Check out this stuff that is about working at the company.'

"And then, over time, maybe the candidate has two bad weeks at work and is suddenly ready to apply for a job. This company is top of mind. And they go back and apply for a job, or a recruiter reaches out to them and says, 'Hey, I know you didn't apply for a job, but we've got something open that's perfect for you. Do you have ten minutes to talk on the phone?' It's the same thing that marketing does. It's just we're taking it to HR because HR needs it."

Next, I asked Phil about his suggestions for what to include in a career page or career site for companies of different sizes—under 100 employees, 100-500 employees, and over 500 employees.

Phil: "When companies are very small, like that 100 stage, I think they just need some basic information on their career website. I think they need a talent community to capture those passive candidates who aren't going to apply. This is especially true for companies that are growing and having lots of press events. Maybe they're raising a new round of funding. That will drive a lot of people to the career website who are not job seekers, that don't have resumes. We need to capture those people.

"They also tend to outsource a lot of their recruiting. If you're spending the 20% or 30% fee from a third-party recruiter every time you hire somebody, that is money that could be pumped back into your business. Having the right career site and talent community will drastically decrease those fees. You can recruit off inbound candidates as opposed to having to pay somebody to go outbound for you.

> Talent Optimizer Tip: Invest in a career site early to generate a stream of inbound candidates.

"I don't think things change too much after you grow beyond 100; the struggles are the same. It will just be amplified more as a 500-person company. As a 100-person company, you want to get the word out about your business. Not as many people know about you, so you will need your employees to post on social media about the company, or maybe do a meetup or have a webinar about what it's like to work at your company. I think the 500-person company should be doing that, too, just on a bigger scale.

"When you get to enterprise, it becomes a bit more complicated. If I'm an organization with more than fifty recruiters, I probably want to have a CRM that is very robust and can track what everybody is doing. I probably want to have more advanced e-mail workflow triggers and stuff like that. I've never seen an organization do that well. I guess that Google and Facebook and Amazon probably do it well. Here in Boston, we have Wayfair, which is a smart team, and I think it will probably get there over the next couple of months. However, I think that it's a really hard thing to do, and even the J.P. Morgans of the world aren't doing it that well."

Phil's company does a great job of helping businesses apply the best strategies from internet marketing to recruiting. Like a true entrepreneur, he identified a gap in the market and set out to fill it with an innovative offering. It's never too early to start building a talent community, and this can be done via an e-mail list or a Facebook or LinkedIn group. The key is to capture interested people with the right values and stay in touch with them.

> Talent Optimizer Tip: It's never too early to start building a talent community. Start with an e-mail list or a Facebook or LinkedIn group.

A Final Note on Sourcing Talent

The best talent will often come from referrals. Referrals are also the most inexpensive way to get high-quality candidates who match your company culture. To generate a consistent flow of quality referrals, follow the above steps to create a custom job posting that polarizes the role. Get specific about the type of person you are looking for, then ask your employees to push out the opportunity on their social media channels. My client, Baro, recently ran another job fair, and employees enthusiastically shared the flyer on their Instagram stories. Other clients share their job posting via LinkedIn using a strategy like the hand-written note posted above. A multipronged approach to talent sourcing is always going to yield the best results. Always keep track of your candidate sources. Measuring this will help you know where to spend your recruiting resources in the future.

Chapter 9 Action Steps

1. Create an About Us page on your website and include your company values and purpose.
2. Identify the social platforms your employees use most.
3. Optimize your personal social profiles.
4. Optimize your company social profiles.
5. Connect to your direct reports, employees, and customers.
6. Create a custom description for every role.
7. Put yourself in the candidate's shoes and don't be afraid to try counter-intuitive approaches for getting your message out.
8. Build your talent pipeline and stay in touch with your talent community.

CHAPTER 10 – THE 5-STEP REFERENCE CHECK

The final step in the recruiting and interview process should always be a reference check. I often observe clients overlook the importance of a structured reference check as they feel it's more of a formality than a necessity.

Here is my five-step reference check system.

First, it's important to let candidates know early on in the interview process that you will be checking references. I like to mention this when I am asking some of the values-based interview questions. I'll say something like, "When I check your references, what are they likely to say about your approach to X?"

Always ask candidates for a minimum of three references for individual contributors and five for managers and above. As you go through the interview process, keep track of the names the candidate mentions in response to your questions. Ask the candidate for specific references. If it is a customer-facing role like sales, be sure to ask for client references in addition to your internal references. If it's an internal manager role, be sure to ask for both the candidate's managers and subordinates. Your goal is to get a well-rounded view of the candidate.

Chapter 10 – the 5-step reference check

Preparing for the Reference Check

Prepare for a reference check as you would an interview. Create your list of structured questions and methodically work your way through them. A thorough reference check will take between thirty and forty-five minutes.

Your job while conducting the reference check is three-pronged.
1. You must validate the information the candidate told you about their work history and performance.
2. You must validate the quality and trustworthiness of the reference.
3. You will want to dig for information that the candidate would not have readily provided to you.

Before you begin each reference call, take a few minutes to look up the reference's Company About Us page if you have not already done so. Try to get a sense of the company culture and working environment. Next check Glassdoor to see if there is anything to note about the culture.

Talent Optimizer Tip: Use a video chat service like Zoom to conduct the reference call. You can record the call for reference later (let the other party know about this). You can also read body language, an incredibly important part of the reference check.

Casey Huebsch is the president and CEO of South End Partners, an executive search firm that focuses on sourcing talent for specialized roles. His team takes a different approach to executive search. They invest heavily in the use of data, analytics, and structured interview scoring to ensure they have the right person for the right role. I've worked with Casey to help refine a structured interview scoring system, and the approach delivers a truly superior quality of candidate-to-company fit when applied consistently.

Casey offered to share his reference questions list with me as an example of how to conduct a thorough and advanced reference check.

Five-Step Reference Check

Step 1 - General Questions

Begin the reference check with a short discussion about the reference's relationship with the candidate. Ask about the candidate's level of experience. Probe to understand how closely they worked together and about the reporting relationship. Next, you will dig into the candidate's work history, confirm the information they gave you during the interview and in their resume. If the candidate mentioned any specific projects or accomplishments, ask the reference to describe these for you. Confirm the impact they had on the performance of the company. In this part, you are listening for consistency. Is the reference telling you a similar story to what the candidate told you? It should be similar, but not too perfect. If it's too perfect, it may have been rehearsed. If you think this is the case, keep probing for additional information, like who else may have been involved in the project or who else you might need to talk to.

Here are some questions for the work history part of the reference check:

- Tell me about your relationship with the candidate.
- What do you remember most about <_Candidate Name_>?
- Please comment on his or her key contributions and accomplishments to your organization. What made these accomplishments important?
- Describe the candidate's work ethic. Listen for hesitation here and dig in if you hear anything other than a glowing endorsement.

Next, you will want to describe the new role for which the candidate is applying and ask the reference about his or her views of the candidate in this role. Probe for desire. Ask, "Will the candidate want to do this job?"

Next, you will follow the Talent Optimizer interview recipe: Ask about values, abilities, and skills.

Step 2 – Culture and Values

Inquire about the corporate culture. Get specific, and probe to understand the values. Ask what makes people a good fit for the culture or what makes people a poor fit. How did the candidate perform in this setting? What made him or her a great fit? Ask for examples. Ask follow-up questions until you have a good sense of the culture and what made the candidate fit or not fit.

In what type of work environment does this person thrive? Please explain. Here you are listening for clues about the level of autonomy and independence or support, degree of structure, the pace of change, etc. Ask follow-up questions and probe until you have a good feel for the environment.

Step 3 – Abilities

How would you describe the candidate's personality?
Ask about each behavioral factor to evaluate alignment to the behavioral assessment results. These questions will help you validate how well the reference knows the candidate. Note the responses for each.

- Is the candidate more assertive or supportive?
- Is the candidate more social and outgoing or private and reflective?
- Is the candidate more driving or patient?
- Is the candidate more flexible or formal?

Predictive Index Behavioral Questions: Dig into the same behavioral fits and gaps addressed with the candidate. If the candidate is low on extraversion and the role requires an outgoing, persuasive style, ask about a situation where the candidate had to demonstrate this. Refer to the behavioral interview questions in chapter 6 for a list of the questions by behavioral drive.

- How does the candidate learn best?
- How quickly does the candidate get up to speed on new things or deal with change? If this is important, ask about a complicated project or situation that required quick learning, have the reference describe it in detail and how the candidate performed.

Step 4 – Skills

Include the most appropriate skills for the role. Your goal here is to validate what the candidate told you in the interview and evaluate them for what you require for the position. Additionally, you are looking to dig for some areas of potential improvement. For leadership roles, this may also include leadership competencies.

Start by asking the reference about any areas the candidate is uniquely strong in and in any areas that the candidate needs improvement. As expected, you will likely not get the needs improvement without probing.

Comment on their skills regarding (enter field) their strengths, with examples.

- For a technical role like a developer, ask about their proficiency in different programming languages. Rate them on a scale of 1-10 for various programming languages. Ask for examples of projects to validate the reference rating.
- For a sales position, ask about the different stages of the sales process. These include generating new opportunities, presenting to clients, closing business, and growing existing accounts. Rate on a scale of 1-10. Ask about some challenging wins; also validate the candidate's track record.
- For administrative roles, you might include a list of required skills such as:
    - Order processing speed and accuracy
    - Client service and communication, written and verbal
    - Organizational skills
    - Computer proficiency by application: Word, Outlook, Salesforce, etc.

If the reference did not rate the candidate a 10, ask what they would need to do to earn a 10.

Forced Ranking Strategy

Casey gave me a great strategy to dig into the candidate's skills using a forced ranking system.

I am going to ask you about some of the required leadership skills and competencies. I'd like you to rate the candidate on a scale of 1-10, but please limit your 10/10 to two of the five.

1. Problem-solving
2. Managing conflict

Chapter 10 – the 5-step reference check

3. Gaining buy-in
4. Driving change
5. Giving presentations

Immediately follow up this question by asking what the candidate would need to demonstrate to earn a 10/10 if they were rated a 9/10 or less.

This strategy can also be used before the call to help you gain some information about the candidate before you speak with the reference. Email them the list of skills a few minutes before the reference call and ask them to rate the candidate on the five skills listed.

Step 5 - Final Questions

Finish off your reference check with a few questions:
1. What have I not asked you about that I should have asked? If you were in my position, what else would you want to know about the candidate?
2. Who else should I speak with?
3. Would you enthusiastically hire this person again? Pay very close attention to voice inflection and body language here, if you sense any hesitation, dig in immediately and don't back down until you find out why.

Reference check summary

Remember your three objectives:
1. Validate the information the candidate told you about their work history and performance.
2. Validate the quality and trustworthiness of the reference.
3. Dig for information that the candidate would not have readily provided to you.

You must treat the reference check like you do an interview. Don't accept answers at face value; ask for specific examples of what the candidate did. Dig to find out what they need to do to improve. Listen for tonality and voice inflection as clues. If you are doing the reference check using Zoom or in person, watch for body language. Take lots of notes, and cross-reference the information provided with other references. This step takes some time, but it is time well spent to avoid surprises down the road.

Chapter 10 Action Steps

1. Create your own reference check question list using the 5-step format above,
    a. General questions
    b. Culture and Values questions
    c. Abilities questions
    d. Skills questions
    e. Final questions

2. Book a meeting to roll this out to managers responsible for hiring.

It always amazes me how few companies take the time to create a custom job posting for every role. Then, they are surprised when they get average or below-average applicants.

Think about the job posting as your first impression on the candidate. Don't you want the candidate reading the job posting to feel like it was written just for them?

CHAPTER 11 – ONBOARDING AND TRAINING

"Train people well enough so they can leave, treat them well enough so they don't want to."
~ Sir Richard Branson

Many companies overlook the importance of a structured onboarding system for new hires. I firmly believe the saying that you only get one chance to make a first impression holds for onboarding new hires. When a new employee walks through the door for the first time, they are still evaluating the company to confirm they made the right decision. In my experience, a poor first impression is one of the leading reasons new hires don't stick with a company. I know because I've seen the effects of a poor onboarding system firsthand many times in my consulting work. Additionally, I regret to say I was even responsible for a few failures in this area early on in my career.

Training or Onboarding?

The first step to an effective onboarding system is to define what counts as onboarding and what activities count as training.

- Onboarding activities cover everything related specifically to your company.

- Training activities cover the job-related skills that an employee needs to perform the job.

I still see many companies using the "tribal method" of training new hires. This method involves the new employee spending time with a more experienced employee to learn by osmosis, as one would have done thousands of years ago in a hunter-gatherer tribe. This tribal method of training is often a mistake. In this chapter I will share some strategies to onboard and train your people.

Use Nudges

For the topic of nudges in the workplace, read *Work Rules!: Insights from Inside Google That Will Transform How You Live and Lead* by Laszlo Bock. Google is always running experiments on their employees to see how they can improve efficiency, health, and wellness.

If you Google "Nudge Theory," you will get this wiki definition: "Nudge theory (or nudge) is a concept in behavioral science, political theory, and economics that proposes positive reinforcement and indirect suggestions to try to achieve non-forced compliance to influence the motives, incentives, and decision-making of groups and individuals."

The concept of a nudge has countless applications in the workplace. I've included it here to help managers do a better job at onboarding.

For this application, let's consider a "nudge" a small signal or reminder in the environment that prompts you to do something.

One of my favorite uses of a nudge for managers was from *Work Rules!* In the pilot project, Google sent reminder emails to managers the Sunday night before new hires started work. These emails noted a simple checklist that detailed what successful managers should do with their new hires:

1. Have a role-and-responsibility discussion.
2. Match your Noogler (New Google employee) with a peer buddy.
3. Help your Noogler build a social network.
4. Set up onboarding check-ins once a month for your

Chapter 11 – Onboarding and Training

Noogler's first six months.

5. Encourage open dialogue.[21]

The results were astounding. The new employees who reported to the managers who received the nudge e-mails became productive 25% faster than their peers. This shortened onboarding by a month in some cases.

 Talent Optimizer Tip: Use Nudge emails to remind managers to cover essential onboarding steps with new hires.

Consider what best practices you would like all of your managers to follow with new hires. Create checklists and give them to your managers. As a rule of thumb, the more formal the person, the more specific the onboarding milestones need to be.

Training

Finding people with a learning mindset is one of the most challenging, but also the most important, things you can do as a leader. Some studies suggest that as much as 90% of the adult workforce will not pursue learning opportunities on their own. This indifference to learning is the reason why almost all professional designations have an ongoing learning requirement. Finding the people who independently enjoy learning is a great way of building a lasting competitive advantage.

I am a firm believer in personal development for both career and personal interest reasons. One of my favorite interview questions is about a book or course the candidate recently completed. Most candidates know to have at least one or two books ready to reference. I'm curious to know what genre they read or study. But it's the follow-up questions that separate the real learners from the posers. I always ask: "So, what did you learn from this book?" Then I ask, "So how did you apply this learning? What difference did it make in your life or job?" See, I don't care what the candidate learned. The part I am interested in is how they applied the learning. Did they do anything with it? Did it make a difference? It's disappointing to report that, in my experience, 95% of people I interview can't give me a basic example of how they learned something and applied it.

Finding people with a learning mindset is the first step. Once you do, you need to give them opportunities to learn, both on the job and personally. According to a Forbes article, one of the top five reasons millennials quit their job is to learn new skills.[22] If you have a team of hungry learners, you need to build in opportunities for learning on an ongoing basis and make it clear to everyone that these opportunities exist and are encouraged.

I once heard a business joke that goes something like the following:

CEO and CFO are discussing the amount of money spent on training employees.

CFO asks CEO: What happens if we spend money training our people, and then they leave?

CEO: What happens if we don't, and they stay?

When positioning training internally, the question of Return on Investment (ROI) always comes up, at some point or another. ROI of training can be challenging to measure because it's difficult to isolate the variables that cause the change. If you conduct a training session right before your busy season, chances are you will see an uptick in results. Was it because of the training or the change in season? Looking at sales year-over-year helps to account for this, but then you need to factor in economic trends and the impact the economy has on results year over year. When it comes to ROI on training, it's essential to consider factors beyond just the investment and its immediate impact on metrics.

- Does your training have an impact on your brand?
- Does your training program help you attract or retain top talent?
- Do you measure the level of skill and knowledge going into the training and after the training?
- Do you use a test-train-retest system?

Who Should Attend Training?

The short answer here is everyone. If you are creating an organization built to last, everyone at every level in the organization

Chapter 11 – Onboarding and Training

should focus on ongoing learning and idea-sharing.

In his timeless masterpiece, *The E-Myth,* Michael Gerber describes the dynamic between management and people. He says there are no real people problems, only management problems, and most management problems are really system problems. I am paraphrasing here, but the point is that most companies don't systemize things to the degree necessary to remove the variability in the way people do most day-to-day things. Thus, if you find that your people are struggling to get things done right, chances are your training program isn't comprehensive enough.

When it comes to training, top-down initiatives work best. There is a story I once heard about a VP sales meeting with a CEO. The CEO asks the VP for his opinion on the new sales training course. The VP says he hasn't heard the feedback yet, and the CEO replies, "You didn't attend the sales training with your team?" The VP says no. The CEO then asks, "How will you know if the sales team is adopting the new strategies if you didn't attend the training?"

This kind of thing, seeing executives sign off on expensive training initiatives but not take the time to attend themselves, befuddles me time and again. If you are training your direct reports, you should at least have a working knowledge of the material. It's exponentially better if you master the material first, allowing you to test and challenge your people after the training. I always like to arrange an executive overview of the material to management about one week before the training event. A one-hour crash course on the key topics and takeaways with the trainer is always a good starting point. It gets me thinking about how the material will apply to the business. It gives me a chance to ask questions and ensure that the material will resonate with my people. Most training organizations will throw this in for free or only charge a nominal amount, especially when the session is held online through Gotomeeting, Zoom, Skype, or Google Hangouts.

New Hire Training vs. Onboarding

I am a member of several CEO and leadership organizations. At a meeting discussing sales training, the topic of training vs. onboarding came up. What is the difference between the two and who owns what?

I think my good friend Michel Falcon does a pretty good job of defining onboarding. He says, "Employee onboarding is the design of what your employees feel, see, and hear after they have been hired."[23]

Designing an onboarding process goes far beyond the first day; it should be a planned process over the first 100 days, with maintenance steps beyond that. An SHRM report notes that "At Corning Glass Works, new employees who attended a structured orientation program were 69% more likely to remain at the company up to three years."[24]

The report further classifies onboarding into four steps, the Four Cs:[25]

1. Compliance is the lowest level and includes teaching employees basic legal and policy-related rules and regulations.
2. Clarification refers to ensuring that employees understand their new jobs and all related expectations.
3. Culture is a broad category that includes providing employees with a sense of organizational norms—both formal and informal.
4. Connection refers to the vital interpersonal relationships and information networks that new employees must establish.

Thinking about onboarding as a separate and distinct step from training can ensure that you don't skip over this vitally important part of the employee lifecycle.

In summary, research on new employee onboarding shows that when onboarding is done correctly, it leads to:

- Higher job satisfaction.
- Organizational commitment.
- Lower turnover.
- Higher performance levels.
- Career effectiveness.
- Lowered stress.

What Type of Training is Needed?

Just like athletes need the practice to stay at the top of their game, regular training is essential to the maintenance of any skill. If you want your organization to run like a finely tuned machine, you must maintain the machine through regular and consistent training.

I believe that, for most roles, you should have at least one

Chapter 11 – Onboarding and Training

regularly scheduled training session. Most employees will look at this as repetitive, but remember: even the world's best golfers spend time on the practice range with a coach to ensure they don't develop bad habits.

When to Hold the Training

Training should take place weekly through both structured assignments and group exercises. Jordan Belfort, famous from the book and movie The Wolf of Wall Street, spent two hours a day training his stockbrokers on sales and closing techniques. He spent one hour at the beginning of the day and one hour at the end, training and re-training everyone in the boardroom of Stratton Oakmont. I am not suggesting that the boiler-room tactics were ethical or legal, but there's no denying that his people were extremely well trained.

Incentives for Learning

I am a big believer in providing incentives for learning, both structured and unstructured. When I ran my first business, I would often provide unexpected bonuses to employees who "got caught doing something right." I'd look for examples of people going above and beyond to satisfy customers or help a colleague.

Case Study Bounties

Offering a structured incentive for case studies is a great way to encourage salespeople to follow up with clients to document the success and ROI of the investment. It will also encourage business development reps to share ideas. This case study strategy works in recruiting, too. These examples will help with training and create an asset for the company in the form of a training process.

Where to Hold the Training

Weekly training is best held on-site, whenever possible. If the team is remote, conducting live-video training via Skype or Google Hangout or Zoom is the next best option. At least once and ideally twice annually, the team should get together outside the office for a structured skills-development retreat.

How Adults Learn

One of the biggest challenges with change is rooted in the way we learn. From a young age, we are taught that learning is measured by knowledge retention, but the results we achieve in the real world are measured by our ability to translate learned knowledge into applications.

Adults learn best through experiential learning, applying the topics live. If your training only tests an employee's ability to recall facts or cite material from an employee handbook, you are missing the point.

How to Facilitate the Training

I believe training can take place in all forms: online, in person, self-study, and group work. The most important thing is to make it repetitive and to assess both knowledge retention and application. At the end of each training session, send out a test or small project to evaluate the team's proficiency. If you are training soft skills like a sales presentation, try recording some of the presentations to create a "how-to" library for new hires.

How to Make Training Stick

"Practice: Adults do best with experiential learning by doing. Practice: Acquiring behavioral skills (versus concepts) requires repetition; people must try a new behavior multiple times (from three to twenty times, according to different studies) before it becomes practiced enough to be comfortable and effective."[26]

Repetition is the key to making training stick—repetition in training and repetition in testing. When coaching my sales teams, we do a quiz or role-play every single week, and every single week we review a topic. I know that most of the reps already know what we are going to cover in the review, but the repetition keeps it on top of their minds and prevents them from developing bad habits.

Chapter 11 Action Steps

Chapter 11 – Onboarding and Training

1. List your onboarding steps.
2. Create a "nudge" reminder for managers to cover the new hire onboarding activities.
3. Document your training programs.
4. For every new hire request, ensure the manager has a documented training plan ready.
5. Try using video recordings of your best employees in action to create a library of how-to resources for new hires.
6. Implement a case study bounty program.

CHAPTER 12 – CULTURE CHAMPIONS

You have hired a great team of like-minded people who believe in a shared cause. Each team member is assigned the type of work that suits their abilities and skills. Now what?

Keeping your culture healthy doesn't happen by accident. Like many other things in life, this is something you should take a proactive approach to support. For this chapter, I spent some time with the team at 360insights. This company uses a forward-thinking approach around culture and engagement. This method has earned the company the title of the number one best place to work in Canada, as named by the Great Place to Work Institute. The company has been ranked in the top four spots for five years running.[27]

The Culture at 360insights

I sat down with Travis Dutka, the company's culture curator, to learn what they do to support their company culture. I met the president and CEO, Jason Atkins, several years ago. Jason suggested I interview Travis to document their unique approach.

Travis came from the nonprofit world, had a stint as a foreign currency trader, and spent some time learning the service industry as a Starbucks barista after graduating from university.

Travis recalled, "One thing I think contributed to where I ended up today is that I've always pursued relationships and meaning or purpose in my work. I wanted to make sure that my work mattered, and I wanted to feel that I was contributing value and doing something important."

As culture curator, Travis oversees everything development-related, from training to figuring out "what does culture mean and how does that integrate it into everything the company does?" From performance reviews to celebrations, to employee engagement, Travis gets to build company culture into everyday life at 360insights.

360insights is an enterprise-level software company that offers full contact support to its customers. As of 2018, the company had about 375 employees globally, with about 285 based out of their head office in Whitby, Ontario.

About a third of the team is in client success or customer support. Another third is technical, software development, and project management on the technical side. The final third is people involved in operations, human resources, marketing, sales, and finance.

Travis joined 360insights in 2012. At that time, the company had been around for about four years. He tells me that "culture has been pretty top of mind from the early days, when our founder and CEO, Jason Atkins, decided to start this company. He came out of a situation that was not ideal. He set out from day one, stating, 'I want to create a company that I want to be at, and I want people to enjoy being at it.'"

Jason's vision was to build the best place to work in the world. To accomplish this, he established three core commitments early on:

1. An unbelievable experience for our clients.
2. An unbelievable place to work for our team.
3. To make a difference in the world.

Travis elaborates: "Those were founding commitments that I talked to our team about as being our compass. A compass tells you where to go. It doesn't tell you how to get there, and it's not a tightrope that you can fall. It just is that guiding star. It's that north star that you can come back to and say, 'Hey, are we doing this? Are we making a difference?' Jason had those in place from day one."

As a next step, the team developed its set of core values before they reached fifty employees. To arrive at their unique core values, the team used a survey asking, 'What values do you have or aspire to live by?' It was a crowdsourcing way of identifying the values that already existed within the team.

"Jason and his chief of staff, Todd Skinner, worked the suggestions down from a big number. All fifty people provided two or three different values. We combined it, put the different values phrases together, and had another vote.

"What they came up with was:
1. Don't find a fault; find a remedy.
2. Live in the possible.
3. Be real and have fun."

Todd and Jason would always tell this story of when they were in on a Saturday. A woman dropped by, trying to sell them something.

They said, "We're just talking about core values."

The salesperson said, "We have core values."

Todd and Jason asked, "What are they?" and the woman said, "I don't know. I think integrity's one of them."

They looked at each other. That was an epiphany for them, when they said, "If our employees are out in the world, and they don't know what our core values are, then we failed as leaders."

They said, "We need to make sure that our values are meaningful, they're relevant, and they're sticky." That's when they came up with the value phrases.

Then a couple of years later, they were speaking with Zappos, which is known for having a really strong corporate culture. They spent some time with one of their culture people while visiting the Zappos head office and doing a tour. Travis explains, "They were pretty impressed with what we had put together, and that we had a culture book, which is like a yearbook of memory, a year in review. We showed them that, and they were excited.

"They said, 'This is really great, but do you have any values around your work, like actually doing good work?'

"We ended up adding a fourth value at that point in time: It's not what you say, it's what you do.

"It was around a commitment to work. We actually added value to the process. I know some companies change their values, and some companies keep them and don't ever change them, but we added to them."

Next, we discussed how 360insights uses the core commitments and core values in action.

Travis had a couple of great analogies: "If the core commitments

Chapter 12 – Culture Champions

are like a compass, the core values to me are like the map. They're more the rules of engagement, and they give examples and the framework for how we interact with each other.

'Don't find a fault, find a remedy' has to do with looking for opportunities and not problems. Having a positive attitude is overcoming challenges. Right off the bat in orientation, every employee goes through a full day that has nothing to do with their job; it has to do with the company. We go through our history. A lot of what we're talking about, that's what we dive into. We look at personal values. We do some conversation with Jason, the CEO. We build that framework, and how people understand the underlying 'why' that we exist, and how we got to where we are. We don't help them do their job better, but that's really important. That's an anchoring point.

Core values, core commitments are elaborated on, and we talk about how we're making a difference in the world, how we view an unbelievable experience for our clients and dig into that a little bit very early on. It used to be day one, but we have so many different starting dates that we typically run it about once a month now. It's like an anchor point; if you can connect people to the why, it's not just a 'punch in-punch out.' They can connect to the vision, and they can add some purpose and meaning to work."

Culture Ambassador Team

360insights has created a culture ambassador team to act as a sounding board for management. Travis describes them as a "voice of the people back to the executive or HR team." The team is entirely volunteer-elected by peer employees; they get voted in once per year. It is responsible for organizing culture events for the company and for working on integrating the values into the business.

One of the first culture ambassador teams helped to define the core values in action. The thinking is that you can't incorporate core values into performance reviews if no one knows how the values look in practice.

Here are the 360insights Core Values defined

Value: Live in the Possible

Definition: Live and work free of limitation.
Specific actions that meet this objective/value:
- Constantly strive for personal and professional improvement
- Enact positive change fearlessly
- Being driven and passionate about what we do
- Beat the odds

Value: Be Real, Have Fun
Definition: Act with integrity while encouraging happiness.
Specific actions that meet this objective/value:
- Smile or laugh while taking on a difficult task (smile, against all odds)
- Speak with confidence about the truth
- Find ways to connect deeply with others regarding happiness (know what makes you happy and what makes others around you happy)
- Open and honest communication – treating others how you would like to be treated
- Create a workplace free of gossip

Value: Don't find a fault; find a remedy
Definition: Focus on creating solutions to problems.
Specific actions that meet this objective/value:
- Take ownership of problems and push through to resolution
- Show poise and think on your feet
- Demonstrate analytical thinking and the ability to pivot mentally
- Think about a solution and the opportunities it may present BEFORE bringing up the problem/challenge

Value: It's not what we say. It's what we do
Definition: Strive for excellence and deliver on your commitments
Specific actions that meet this objective/value:
- Be accountable
- Keep your promises
- Set goals and crush them (setting them isn't enough)

- Actions speak louder than words – what we do shows everyone who and what we are

Evaluate Both the How and the What

At 360insights, you are evaluated by your peers and manager, and you conduct a self-review of how you're performing in your tasks, and how well you're living the organization's values.

Each value is broken down, and there is a rating scale. Then there is some discussion around: "Why is that going on?" or "How is that going on?"

The objective of this method is to connect performance and values. With this evaluation system, you can't be amazing at your job and not live the values at all and still get promoted. You can't be amazing at living the values and suck at your job and get promoted either.

Employees are taught that performance at 360insights equals the how and the what. Performance reviews actually say: "Performance equals how and what." If you do terribly on the values, but amazingly technically, you still end up with an average score.

Travis explains that this is often hard for some people to grasp because a lot of employees are wired into the Western view of business. Methods of evaluation and top-grading are drilled into us through school from a young age, and we're all focused on the what—did I get the right answer, did I accomplish the task? This mindset carries over to evaluating employees, evaluating peers, even evaluating how we think about ourselves. Did I do my job? We don't often think about how I did my job. Did I keep relationships intact? Did I build those things that are important to long-term success? Did I get it done?

Travis admits that it's "a real big struggle because it's not how people seem to be wired. It's something that we continually put in there so that we have the discussion." They constantly train managers on how to have that discussion: "You're doing your job well, but your attitude is impacting the team."

Building Strong Personal Relationships

Studies consistently show that employees with strong personal relationships are more engaged and productive than those without strong relationships at work.

In the book, *12: The Elements of Great Managing,* by Rodd Wagner and James K. Harter, the authors identify twelve elements that lead to high levels of employee engagement. The tenth is: "I have a best friend at work."

360insights has several ways of intentionally encouraging employees to develop strong personal relationships.

360 Houses

The company developed 360 Houses about four years earlier. Travis explained, "It's just like Harry Potter, or house league. Red, yellow, green, and blue. We named them. We have coats of arms. We have lanyards. When new hires start—part-time, full-time, coop, students, doesn't matter—they get to pick out of a . . . It's actually a shark. They pick out of a shark, and they get assigned to a house. There's a private #Slack channel for that house. Slack is an internal communication tool. There are little things, from a pumpkin-carving competition to "wear blue to support autism awareness," and you get house points. Once a quarter, there's a winner. The team that wins gets to have a pizza party lunch with the CEO.

That was birthed out of the desire to help people connect with others outside of their department. You typically work with five to ten people on a day-to-day basis. You leave your area to go to the washroom or get coffee, but as we continue to grow really quickly, we lose touch with a lot of people. We thought: if we could help people connect not on their work level, not on their team level, but across the company, we would help them build stronger connections. We have people in the contact center who know software developers, and it's through their houses. You see the lanyard, and you're like, "Hey, you're yellow." Now, even with our offices that are in the US, people get really excited about their houses. Like, "What house are you in?"

By itself, it's not the only answer to connect people across the company, but it is another reference point that can start conversations. It helps remove barriers for shy people. It can put people in the same room for the pizza party—people who'd never necessarily be in the same room because they're in their own big groups. Now they're with a quarter of the company in a room and have a chance to meet."

House Competitions

360insights has a lot of house challenges. One of them is Quarterly Madness. Anyone can challenge anybody to do something and get points for it. It could be a marshmallow-eating or a rock-paper-scissors contest, and you have to find one person from each house to compete. It might also be a free-throw competition in the company gym. There's a lot of little things like this that happen throughout the month, and they're a great way to get people together to meet. Travis stated, "We always take a group photo with the house for a 'culture yearbook,' which we create annually to capture the great experiences the employees had that support the culture."

House Slack Channels

360insights uses Slack channels for both working groups and houses. In the Slack channel, employees have their house color as a way to connect with others from their house. Employees use Slack to arrange carpool rides or ask if anyone knows a good babysitter. The house channels do not have to be work-related; they are there for the employees to use as they like.

Wheel of Lunch

The Wheel of Lunch program is another way employees are connected at 360insights. Each week, on Monday, the culture team pulls three names out of a hat, and those three employees book a day to go out for lunch, paid for by the company. The rules are:
1. You've got to take a selfie.
2. You've got to go within walking distance.
3. You've got to go this week.

The group gets 60 dollars from petty cash to go out for lunch. They focus on connecting. People talk to whomever—a manager and an entry-level employee—it's whatever names come up. The focus is on fostering connection. This is a relatively inexpensive way for three employees to connect outside the office. They learn about new roles, discover common interests, and build bonds with people they might not otherwise have met. Wheel of Lunch works best for groups of up to about 150 employees, so all the employees are included each year. Beyond 150, it's best to create multiple concurrent programs.

> Talent Optimizer Tip: Create a #Companywheeloflunch on Instagram or the company Slack channel for the selfies and include the photos in the annual culture yearbook.

Travis mentioned all sorts of stories and common interests that were identified at the Wheel of Lunch, from a love for cats to RC Car racing.

The Wheel of Lunch generates real business value, too. In one example, someone met with a manager and learned they both had a teaching background. They started putting some internal training together. It was just a random Wheel of Lunch interaction that developed into a valuable business relationship. It didn't lead to a full role change, but it did lead to someone being able to leverage their expertise in the organization.

360 Clubs

360 Clubs are all employee-led clubs. Any employee can start a club and, so long as they can get at least five people together, they get $10 per person per month to get together. The objective here is, again, to help employees identify common interests and build stronger personal relationships outside of work.

Current clubs include a coffee club, a bowling club, a whiskey club, a beer club, a wine club, a sushi club, a scrapbooking club, a journaling club, a card sharks poker club, a board-game club, and an outdoor adventure club.

Each group uses its $10 per person very differently. The scrapbooking club uses it to buy scrapbooking supplies, and the members build their scrapbooks together, sharing tools that they buy by leveraging group economies of scale. The Outdoor Adventure Group uses the money to pay for parking to go for hikes on Saturdays. The wine club uses it to buy bottles of wine that people

Chapter 12 – Culture Champions

wouldn't get on their own, like a $60 curiosity everyone wants to try.

The clubs are completely employee-driven, the company does not put a lot of administrative power behind them, and they come and go according to demand. If the bowling club only wants to bowl in the winter months, it simply falls off over the summer. If people are passionate about a club, it keeps going; if not, it dies off.

Another great benefit of the club format is that it doesn't force people to participate in company events that don't interest them. Running big events can be good for morale, but it's impossible to please everyone. No matter what the event or topic, some people will love it, others will hate it. This gives employees the power to do things they are passionate about.

> "By investing in people's passion, they see that they are important enough to you to be invested in. In return, they give their best back to the company."
> ~Travis Dutka

What's the ROI in all of this culture investment?

The 360 team admits it can be hard to measure ROI directly. But there are several real areas where this does provide a tangible return.

Retention

360insights has some of the lowest turnover rates in the industry. CEO Jason Atkins explained that typical turnover rates in a call-center environment are 35-45% per year; at 360, they have turnover below 10%. Using the estimate of one-times base salary, that works out to about $30,000 per employee saved.

If the fifty-employee call center has an industry-standard turnover of around 40% per year, this would cost the company $600,000 per year in turnover costs.

If the company achieves a 10% turnover rate in the same call center, this works out to $150,000 in turnover costs, a savings of $450,000.

With even the conservative estimate of 1/10th, in the above example, the $45,000 in savings would easily cover the costs of all the company culture programs combined.

Personal Growth and Development

When people are growing personally, they are more engaged. People love teaching what they are passionate about. As Dan Pink identified in his book, Drive, mastery is one of the three components of personal satisfaction. When people are leading clubs, they get to learn about, share, and teach topics about which they are passionate. It allows everyone to showcase something they are great at. There's a real sense of value and worth that you bring to the organization.

Networking

Employees get to network, which ties into retention and growth. They also learn a lot about other employees and departments. Employees get exposed to people and areas of the business where they might find a passion and an interest in developing that passion.

Identifying Future Leaders

Travis believes you can start to see leaders develop: "We haven't officially found a direct correlation between people who start clubs and people being groomed in succession planning, but you do start to see people surface who take the initiative, who run things effectively, who have influence. Because there's positional leadership and influential leadership. You start to see who are the influencers in the organization. They impact culture in a huge way."

Lower Recruiting Costs

Great culture leads to great employees referring other great employees. It's no secret that one of the best sources of future great employees are the existing ones you have today. Referrals are easy when people feel a part of something is important. Additionally, awards like the number-one best place to work in Canada by the Great Place to Work Institute and outstanding online reviews on sites like Glassdoor get 360insights a slew of unsolicited applications. These awards significantly lower recruiting costs for the organization.

The sum of the culture initiatives at 360insights is telling. The company has some of the highest engagement levels I've ever seen. The industry-low turnover results are outstanding. The companies list of awards is impressive, and the cost savings generated are substantial. If you are looking for similar results, consider

Chapter 12 – Culture Champions

implementing some of the above initiatives.

Get Caught Doing Something Right

My father, Stephen Friday, taught me a strategy that I still use to reward people for doing great work. In the late 1980s, my dad was the owner and president of a company that pioneered the credit-card travel rewards programs for the large banks in Canada. The main focus of his business was keeping the bank's customers happy. When he bought the company from its previous owners, his most significant focus was service quality improvement. He implemented a variety of systems to improve quality, and these are still some of the best methods I've seen for supporting and rewarding exceptional performance.

The first was what he called, "Get caught doing something right." In short, he would walk around the call-center floor with a pocket full of $100 bills. When he caught someone doing an exceptional job or going above and beyond to create a great customer experience, he would drop a C-note on their desk. As an employee, you never knew when you were going to get rewarded, but you always knew that you might. The effect this type of random chance reward system has on the brain is similar to that of gambling at a slot machine.

Mariano Choliz published an article in The Journal of Gambling Studies.[28] In the background of the paper, Choliz outlines the reasons slot machines can be so addictive to humans. The first is that they operate on a random payout schedule, but they appear to be on a variable payout schedule. Random payouts fool the players' brains into thinking the more they play, the more they'll win.

Because the employees don't know when they are going to get the reward, they become conditioned to pursue it at all times. What was the result in the aforementioned case? It was great for energizing the floor, and employees were always looking for opportunities to go above and beyond in the creation of exceptional customer experiences. I love these kinds of random rewards because they don't develop a feeling of entitlement, and in my experience, they are more effective than "if, then" rewards.

The second thing he did was install a large wheel-of-fortune-style spinner on the wall in the boardroom. When employees did something exceptional, they got to spin the wheel. The wheel had about thirty prizes, and the prizes were substantial—things like a week of paid vacation, a trip for two to the Caribbean, cash bonuses of $500 to $2,500, new color televisions, etc. My dad recalls, "The wheel was huge, about five feet in diameter, and it made an absolute racket when we spun it, so everyone knew when someone got rewarded." I love this idea because this reward system takes advantage of Pavlovian conditioning. The sound of the spinning wheel creates an anticipation of a reward. Whenever employees heard the wheel spinning, they knew someone was getting a reward, and it created an environment in which everyone was always looking for opportunities to go above and beyond.

You can use this technique to reward all kinds of initiatives. If you have a new quality-improvement or sales initiative, the reward is a spin of the wheel. When new employees finish training and get an exceptional rating on a training program, the managers reward them with a spin of the wheel. It's a great way to build excitement, make the rewards front and center, and get everyone in the office energized about doing something right.

Creating Culture Champions

Another creative way to support corporate culture, reward employees, and build a training library is to create a weekly culture champions program. Here, a culture champion is nominated each week for exemplifying one of the core values. This program works best if the CEO or top local leader goes first. They should observe their people working for a week, and when they catch someone doing something above and beyond that demonstrates one of the core values, they should nominate that employee as the "culture champion of the week." The employee gets a prize or reward for being nominated—it might be a fifty-dollar gift card, a case of beer, or a spin of a wheel, like in my father's company. The person who observed the core value in action must provide a short write-up that explains why the nominated employee deserves to be the culture champion of the week. The write-up gets posted in the company's Slack channel under #culturechampions and in a Word or Google Doc for later use. At the end of the year, create a culture yearbook with fifty-two stories of your values in action.

Chapter 12 – Culture Champions

 Talent Optimizer Tip: Give new employees a copy of the previous year's culture yearbook during onboarding. It's a great way to help them get to know the culture and their new colleagues.

I invite you to share your experiences with me using these strategies under the hashtag #culturechampions on Instagram, submit them at www.robfriday.com.

The Values 360 Scorecard

Building on the performance evaluations at 360insights, I believe evaluating adherence to core values is a great way to sustain the culture — reward employees for not just what they do but how they do it.

I am currently working on a web application to help companies with this feedback-and-tracking program. If you are interested in being a part of the beta testing group, please check www.robfriday.com for details.

The Values 360 scorecard is designed to gather self-assessment, direct-report, peer, and manager feedback related to values.

The Values 360 assessment is a multiplier score applied to a performance score for the employee. Companies can use this process to determine who gets rewarded, promoted, or, in some cases, fired.

Use this formula to track overall performance.
- Overall Performance = W * H
- W represents "What" the employee accomplished
- H represents "How" the employee accomplished it

The What

Each role should have a list of objective outcomes for each quarter. There are many methods for making performance quantifiable. I often recommend the scorecard system from the Entrepreneurial Operating System (EOS) Method as outlined in *Traction* by Gino Wickman.

If an employee accomplishes all objectives for the quarter, they receive a 100% rating on "what "they accomplished.

Next, multiply the 100% rating by the Values 360 score of "How" they accomplished their objectives.

The How

If, for example, a sales rep achieves their sales target, but did a terrible job of interacting with the operations team, they might receive a low total performance rating.

Each value is broken down into its behavioral sub-components. Each organization will define its values differently, so this will take some upfront work.

For example: Suppose ABC Corp is a Web Development and Hosting Company

They have the following six values:
1. Be a lifelong learner
2. Accountability
3. Coachability
4. Be obsessed with service
5. Be in it to win it
6. Celebrate wins

The Values 360 scorecard will break down the types of behaviors and actions that exemplify each value.

Please rate yourself or the employee in question on the following values. One is the lowest possible score. Ten is the highest possible score.

1. **Be a lifelong learner—We take personal responsibility for our learning. We believe in lifelong learning and development, both personally and professionally. Average Score___/10**

Employee takes the initiative to develop new skills or areas of expertise
1 2 3 4 5 6 7 8 9 10

Employee has read a business book or taken a course this quarter

Chapter 12 – Culture Champions

1 2 3 4 5 6 7 8 9 10

Employee applies new knowledge or skills at work or takes the initiative to teach others.
1 2 3 4 5 6 7 8 9 10

2. **Accountability—We take personal responsibility for our actions, outcomes, and deliverables. Average Score____/10**

Employee sets challenging goals and takes personal responsibility for outcomes.
1 2 3 4 5 6 7 8 9 10

Employee meets agreed-upon commitments to others
1 2 3 4 5 6 7 8 9 10

Employee clearly and objectively communicates outcomes and deliverables.
1 2 3 4 5 6 7 8 9 10

Employee demonstrates an internal locus of control and actively takes steps to correct issues.
1 2 3 4 5 6 7 8 9 10

3. **Coachability—We graciously accept coaching and demonstrate a desire to learn from and teach others. Average Score____/10**

Employee graciously accepts coaching and demonstrates new behaviors as a result of coaching feedback.
1 2 3 4 5 6 7 8 9 10

Employee demonstrates a willingness and desire to learn from others.
1 2 3 4 5 6 7 8 9 10

Employee acts as a coach to others.
1 2 3 4 5 6 7 8 9 10

4. **Be obsessed with service**—We are obsessed with going above and beyond to improve the condition of others. Average Score____/10

Employee demonstrates a "giving" mindset.
    1   2   3   4   5   6   7   8   9   10

Employee goes above and beyond to deliver excellent service to customers and/or other employees.
    1   2   3   4   5   6   7   8   9   10

Employee demonstrates a desire to create raving fans of the company and brand.
    1   2   3   4   5   6   7   8   9   10

5. **Be in it to win it** – We always strive to be #1 in everything we do. We do not compromise on quality, and we are always striving to deliver outstanding results. Average Score____/10

Employee demonstrates a desire to perform at their personal best.
    1   2   3   4   5   6   7   8   9   10

Employee's performance positively impacts the overall team performance.
    1   2   3   4   5   6   7   8   9   10

Employee consistently delivers a winning performance and does not settle for average outcomes.
    1   2   3   4   5   6   7   8   9   10

6. **Celebrate wins** – We work hard, and we play hard. We celebrate victories as a team. Average Score____/10

Employee celebrates wins with the team.
    1   2   3   4   5   6   7   8   9   10

Chapter 12 – Culture Champions

Participates in team activities.
1   2   3   4   5   6   7   8   9   10

Employee celebrates the wins of other employees.
1   2   3   4   5   6   7   8   9   10

Calculate the average score from each category. Calculate the total score and average it to arrive at your overall values score.

Calculate the Values 360 scores from all other raters. The total score is either averaged or scored using a weighing scale, and the result is your "How" multiplier.

The average score is arrived at by taking the average of all the scores gathered.

Apply a weighting to the scores such as:
- 20% self-score
- 30% manager score
- 20% average peer score
- 30% average direct report scores.

For best results, include evaluations from the employee, peers, direct reports, and manager. The Values 360 captures a full 360-view of how the employee lives the core values.

Once my Values 360 assessment is ready, it will also be able to identify blind spots. For example, the employee may rate themselves very highly on coachability, but their manager may rate them lower. This negative blind spot indicates an area of potential development.

The benefit of creating an average score for each of the individual values is that it allows you to identify if an employee severely lacks in one area.

Additionally, by scoring each value independently, a company may elect to apply a weighting scale to the values.

Finally, some organizations may have additional table-stakes values with binary scoring. These are not core values, but values by which all organizations should strive to live.

For example:

Acts with honesty and integrity: YES / NO

Treats all fellow employees with respect: YES / NO

If an employee receives a NO on a table-stakes value, they are given a month to correct the issue. Some companies will have a three-strike rule here; others will have a probation and termination rule.

Chapter 12 Summary

Travis made one additional point in our interview. He believes culture is all about "being intentional." We have a multitude of suggestions outlined above. My recommendation to you is to select the items you believe you have the bandwidth to implement now.

Most importantly, create your core values' 360 scorecard and define what they look like in action. If you are serious about building a values-driven organization, you must create a feedback loop to reinforce the core values regularly. Give employees feedback in private when they are not meeting the values and praise them in public when they do. Find creative ways to share the wins and make sure everyone understands expectations.

Chapter 12 Action Steps

1. Create a culture committee or culture ambassador team.
2. Create "houses" with Slack channels.
3. The Wheel of Lunch.
4. Create a "culture yearbook."
5. Institute weekly or monthly Culture Champion Award + Write-ups.
6. Get caught doing something right.
7. Introduce the Big Wheel of Rewards.
8. Fund employee-led company clubs.

Call to Action

How do you support culture at your organization? Email me with your ideas for a chance to be featured in the next edition of Talent Optimizer. Submit your story at www.robfriday.com

Creating Culture Champions

Interested in implementing the weekly or monthly culture champion program? Share your culture champion stories with the #talentoptimizer for a chance to be featured on my social media and in follow-up to Talent Optimizer.

CHAPTER 13 – TALENT OPTIMIZER RECRUITING

I have one word to describe what separates the companies that succeed with this system from those that don't: consistency.

Consistently implementing these practices and adhering to the processes outlined in these chapters is what will make the difference in your business.

As I stated in Chapter 1, the talent optimizer process is not about doing thousands of things—it's about consistently doing a few things very well. Consistency allows you to scale, to measure, and identify trends. Consistency will enable you to improve and methodically get better each week, month, quarter, and year.

In this chapter, I will outline the steps to apply the talent optimizer process to recruiting.

The Typical Recruiting Process

In my experience, the average organization's recruiting process resembles something like the following.

Step 1 - Job Posting
   Most organizations start with a generic job posting, often using a cut and paste from similar jobs at the company or, worse, similar

positions from a job site like Indeed. They describe the role, focusing on the briefcase requirements: knowledge, skills, and experience. The company description is generic, focusing on what the company does.

Candidates are instructed to apply through a job application link or to email a resume and cover letter to the hiring manager or HR business partner overseeing the job search.

Step 2 - Resume Screen

The hiring manager or HR business partner familiar with the job screens the resumes. The resume screener short-lists for phone screens based on the briefcase assets.

Step 3 – Phone Screen

The hiring manager or HR business partner phone screens. They focus the conversation on what the job is about and what the company does. They ask questions about the candidate's level of experience, qualifications for the job, and salary expectations.

Step 4 – Interview(s)

The hiring manager or HR business partners conduct one or two interviews. The interview structure is ad hoc, often focusing on a discussion of recent experience and a resume walk-through. The interviewer evaluates the interviewee based on their subjective opinion of how much they "liked" the candidate.

Step 5 – Interview Feedback Compiled

The interviewer compiles feedback, and the hiring manager makes a decision.

Step 6 – Reference Check

Reference checks are often skipped. If a reference check is conducted, it is often generic in nature and does not cover specific areas of concern. Candidates are given the option of whom they provide as references.

Step 7 – Final Decision

The hiring manager makes the final decision.

Step 8 – Human Resources Offer
Human resources contact the candidate with an offer of employment.

Several issues arise when using the process outlined above. Most importantly, there is very little structure, and decision-making is very subjective in nature. The candidate's experience will be inconsistent. There is a high probability of unconscious bias. There is no structured method for objectively scoring the quality of responses and thus, no way to measure the effectiveness of the process.

The Talent Optimizer Recruiting Process

Here is a sample of a structured recruiting process with specific measurables at each step.

Step 1— Job Posting
Create a customized job posting with specific behavioral language to attract the right type of candidate. Include a few points about the company culture and the company's purpose and values in the company description. Only include the essential briefcase requirements.

Step 2 — Candidate Applies for Job
The candidate applies, after which, an email auto-responder sends the candidate the culture document explaining the company's purpose and core values.
They then ask the candidate to reply by email with their reaction to the culture document. The candidate is then asked why the company's purpose is important to them, and to rate their core values in order of importance, providing a rationale for their selections.

Step 3 – Application Screen
Someone familiar with all jobs (not just the one for which the candidate applied) screens the resume and culture document responses. If the candidate does not seem like a culture fit, eliminate them from the hiring process. If the candidate is a culture fit, schedule a phone/video interview. Keep all culture fit

resumes on file.

Step 4 – Phone/Video Interview

Schedule a remote interview with the candidate and your HR business partner or hiring manager. Conduct the interview using an online video platform such as Skype, Google Hangouts, Facebook video chat, or something similar. Ask your culture questions, and discuss the candidate's responses to the culture document. Ask the candidate about their value ratings: Why did they select their first choice? Why did they rate their last choice as such? If the candidate passes this screening step, notify them about the next steps in the interview process, including the behavioral and cognitive assessments.

Step 5 – Administer Behavioral and Cognitive Assessments

Step 6 – Structured Interview (ideally in person at the company office)

Budget at least one hour for the interview with the hiring team and twenty minutes for the meeting with the cross-functional teams.

Methodically work your way through your interview scorecard, documenting and scoring all answers. Begin the interview with a review of the candidate's behavioral assessment results. Ask the candidate your structured interview questions designed to address behavioral fits and gaps related to the role. Probe the candidate on the gaps to determine if they have demonstrated a past ability to overcome the differences. Ask the candidate your values questions. Finish this portion of the interview with your desire and work values questions.

Next, have a cross-functional team member interview the candidate to further assess for culture fit.

Step 7 – Skills Test, Assignment, or Presentation

This step will vary depending on the role in question.
- For marketing and creative roles, use a case study or assignment, such as a take-home assignment.
- For accounting and finance roles, use a sample case study and skills test.

- For sales roles, I recommend that the candidate provide a sales presentation. The presentation does not need to be on your product or service; allow the candidate to present something they are comfortable selling. If they are new to sales, ask them to do their best with selling you something basic, like what they had for lunch or the famous pen from The Wolf of Wall Street. Roleplay the sales presentation with them. Be sure to let the candidate know ahead of time to prepare for this—you are not evaluating their ability to make things up on the spot. You are evaluating their ability to ask effective questions and communicate clearly in a live situation.
- For skilled labor, have your on-staff expert administer a skills test. If no expert exists, use your network to find an expert to assist with this evaluation.
- For computer-development roles, have the candidate solve sample coding problems.
- For administrative roles, I recommend a combination of computer-proficiency testing, a words-per-minute typing test, and a sample assignment such as formatting a presentation for consistency and accuracy.

Step 8 – Structured Reference Check

Ask the candidate to provide specific references. Conduct the reference checks yourself, or use someone internal to your company trained on your structured reference checking process.

Step 9 – Combine the Interview Scorecards

Hiring committee and senior leader(s) review scores and collectively make the hiring decision.

Step 10 – Offer of Employment

The hiring team collectively extends the offer of employment, ideally via speakerphone or video call.

Each company's structure will be unique, and the process should allow for adjustments depending on the role and level of seniority. For example, a management role may also require a step to evaluate the candidates' ability to conduct a productive meeting or coaching session. The goal here is consistency. By developing, documenting, and scoring each step, your organization will be prepared to scale by hiring high-quality people with the right values, abilities, and skills.

Hiring Scorecards

At this point, you should have a clear understanding of the Talent Optimizer process and the steps you must take to screen for and hire top-quality talent. I fully recognize that not all organizations will be ready to adopt the complete Talent Optimizer process right away. With that in mind, I am providing two examples of a structured hiring scorecard system: a simple scorecard and an advanced scorecard. As with anything, the more data you track, the more information you will have to make future decisions. The advanced scorecard is preferable, but only if you can stick to it consistently.

Simple Hiring Scorecard for Sales Role

The simple scorecard breaks the interview scoring system into four categories. Depending on the role and situation, you may elect to weight the categories differently. In this example, I have used a 25% weighting value for each category. Each area has a subset of questions with a structured scoring system to help the interviewer evaluate the quality of responses.

Simple Interview Scorecard

Culture fit questions ___/10 Core Values questions ___/10 Attitude___ /5	_____/25
Cognitive Ability – Candidate Score subtracted from Target Score and converted to % match. Max: 100%.	_____/25
Behavioral Fit to Role – Behavioral fit to role based on assessment score /10 Answers to behavioral interview questions___ /15	_____/25
Sales & Presentation Skills Sales questioning skills ___/15 Presentation and communication skills ____/10*	_____/25
Passed Reference Check	**Yes / No**
Total Score	_____**/100**
Recommendation:	

Chapter 13 – Talent Optimizer Recruiting

Advanced Interview Scorecard

Company purpose – Candidate demonstrates an interest and passion for the industry. Provides examples of why the company purpose is meaningful to their personal purpose.	_____/10
Personal Motivation and Drive – Demonstrates a passion for winning, has concrete examples of past top-tier performance and perseverance in the face of rejection or initial failure. Includes score for Desire and Work Values Questions.	_____/10
Company Values Fit – See Values Questions 1. Be a lifelong learner __/5 2. Accountability__/5 3. Coachability__/5 4. Be obsessed with service__/5 5. Be in it to win it__/5 6. Celebrate wins__/5	_____/30
Cognitive Ability – Candidate Score subtracted from Target Score and converted to % match. Max: 100%.	_____/20
Behavioral Fit to Role (optionally weighted by factor importance) Fit score ____/10 Answers to behavioral interview questions ___/10	_____/20
Sales & Presentation Skills Sales questioning skills ____/5 Presentation and communication skills ____/5*	_____/10
Passed Reference Check	**Yes / No**
Total Score	_____/100
Recommendation:	

CHAPTER 14 – GETTING STARTED

The cover of this book made a promise to explain why some companies always get great people. Over the past 13 chapters, I have given you the systems and strategies you will need to get great people. The one thing that causes most leaders to fail at this is consistency. If you take these systems to heart and truly implement them in a real and honest way, they will work for you as they have worked for many others. If you aren't getting the results you want, it's likely one of two reasons. You haven't used the process long enough, or you are not authentic about your core values.

To get started, use the Talent Optimizer Organizational Checkup offered at the end of Chapter 1. Use this scorecard as your baseline to track your progress as you implement the Talent Optimizer process. I encourage you to download the scorecard at www.robfriday.com/TOcheckup

It's also a good idea to get your employees and leaders to complete the scorecard as an internal assessment of your progress.

When starting, I find it is best to set a plan in place and follow the chapters in this book as your guide. I have designed the book as a step-by-step road map to help you build your high-performance organization from the ground up. Start with your purpose, so you know where you are going personally and professionally. Next, work with your leadership team to define your organizational purpose and ensure it has aspirational meaning to your people. Follow this by

Chapter 14 – Getting Started

defining your culture with real, honest, and meaningful core values. Copywrite your core values in a language that speaks your unique culture. Provide your people with examples of what it means to live the core values. Use these core values to ensure you get the right people for your company. Next, it's time to implement a behavioral assessment and skills testing solution to ensure you put the right people in the right roles.

Once you have these steps in place and onboard, train your people. Give them metrics that connect them to the organization's purpose, thus completing the Talent Optimizer process.

Be sure to visit my website and join the Talent Optimizer community on Facebook and LinkedIn. My goal with this community is to help connect like-minded, people-focused leaders to create a more engaging work environment for millions of people. I am always happy to connect.

For speaking, training, and talent optimization consulting inquiries, please visit www.robfriday.com

ABOUT THE AUTHOR

Rob Friday is a Talent Optimization consultant, Author, and Predictive Index® Certified Partner, and trainer. Over the past 10+ years, Rob has worked with hundreds of companies and taught the science of Talent Optimization to over 1000 leaders. Recognized as the fastest-growing partner in Canada in 2018, and a top Predictive Index® Certified Partner globally. Rob is a frequent speaker at trade associations, Fortune 500 companies, and top MBA programs. Today, Rob spends his time helping companies unlock the true potential of their people by implementing the Talent Optimizer process and Predictive Index® systems.

About the Author

[1] http://www.ncsl.org/research/labor-and-employment/national-employment-monthly-update.aspx
[2] http://blog.indeed.com/2017/06/29/trends-job-tenure/
[3] http://blog.indeed.com/2017/06/29/trends-job-tenure/
[4] https://hbr.org/2015/03/technology-can-save-onboarding-from-itself
[5] The survey was conducted online by Harris Poll from August 16 to September 15, 2017, and included a representative sample of 2,257 full-time hiring managers and human resource professionals and 3,697 full-time workers across industries and company sizes in the US private sector. http://press.careerbuilder.com/2017-12-07-Nearly-Three-in-Four-Employers-Affected-by-a-Bad-Hire-According-to-a-Recent-CareerBuilder-Survey
[6] https://business.linkedin.com/content/dam/me/business/en-us/talent-solutions/resources/pdfs/2016-global-talent-trends-v4.pdf
[7] https://www.servantleadershipinstitute.com/what-is-servant-leadership-1/
[8] https://jobs.netflix.com/culture
[9] https://www.zappos.com/about/purpose
[10] The 5 Whys technique was developed and fine-tuned within the Toyota Motor Corporation as a critical component of its problem-solving training
[11] *Who:* The A Method for Hiring by Geoff Smart and Randy Street
[12] Original author unknown, image from "Kaninchen und Ente" ("Rabbit and Duck") from the October 23, 1892, issue of *Fliegende Blätter*
[13] Ray Dalio, *Principles*
[14] The Science Behind PI® Whitepaper
[15] Angela Duckworth, *Grit:* The Power of Passion and Perseverance
[16] https://leadershippipelineinstitute.com
[17] This job posting is partially adapted from the example *in The Ultimate Sales Machine* by Chet Holmes.
[18] American Trucking Association's "Driver Shortage Report 2017
[19] Bureau of Labor Statistics
[20] This "stadium pitch" concept is loosely adapted from *The Ultimate Sales Machine,* by Chet Holmes
[21] Laszlo Bock, Work Rules!: Insights from Inside Google That Will Transform How You Live and Lead, p. 295
[22] https://www.forbes.com/sites/datafreaks/2017/08/22/the-top-5-reasons-millennials-quit-jobs-they-like/#69f15c453df4
[23] http://www.michelfalcon.com/employee-onboarding/
[24] https://www.shrm.org/foundation/ourwork/initiatives/resources-from-past-initiatives/Documents/Onboarding%20New%20Employees.pdf
[25] https://www.shrm.org/foundation/ourwork/initiatives/resources-from-past-initiatives/Documents/Onboarding%20New%20Employees.pdf
[26] http://www.harvardbusiness.org/blog/how-ld-can-accelerate-sales-performance
[27] https://360insights.com/about-us/life360/
[28] https://link.springer.com/article/10.1007%2Fs10899-009-9156-6

Made in the USA
Monee, IL
27 April 2021